Lost Lake

Folk Opera

December 2014   Volume 2 Number 2

In This Issue

Actor, director, playwright, humorist and certified expatriate, **Dan Coffey** ruminates on American culture and celebrity in this satiric fragment from his forthcoming novel.

George W. Bush, Donald Rumsfeld and Dick Cheney were hanging out near the bar. Hillary Clinton and Condoleezza Rice entered the room dressed in tennis clothes and holding rackets.

Minneapolis author, **William E. Burleson**, will take you for a wild ride on a stolen bicycle.

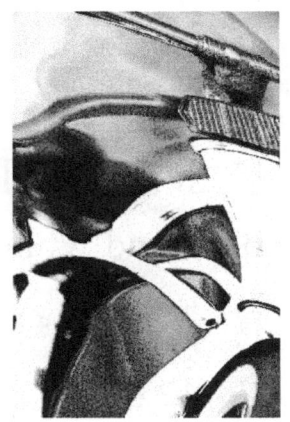

Instead of wisely running away, I swung the sort-of metallic green Cannondale mountain bike up over my head and started running down the street. After a quarter block, I looked back and saw a seemingly endless stream of white guys coming out of the business, all wearing Karate uniforms and pointing at me. I guess it was a Dojo. Who knew? The students started running after me and were gaining fast as I ran down the street with the bicycle over my head.

Arpeggio and Cinquain 34

Morgan Grayce Willow, author of several books of poetry, including *Crossing that Bridge* and *Arpeggio of Appetite*, provides a sampler of measured verse in the Cinquain form.

Punishment 48

Chapter adapted from the novel, *The Sailing Master, Book One: Coming of Age*, by Minneapolis author **Lee Henschel Jr.** whose previous work includes *Short Stories of Vietnam*.

Short Fiction & Novel Fragments

Poetry

Scripts

Folk Opera Photo Essay

Everybody Has One

Discerning readers shop online at www.shipwrecktbooks.com

Lost Lake Folk Opera

Lost Lake Folk Opera is a Shipwreckt Books imprint published twice annually.

P.O. Box 20	Lanesboro, Mn 55949
507 458 8190	contact@shipwrecktbooks.com
Managing Editor	Tom Driscoll
Publisher	Beth Stanford

www.shipwrecktbooks.com

Cover art and interior graphics by Shipwreckt Books

Frogtown Multicultural Fair

By William E Burleson

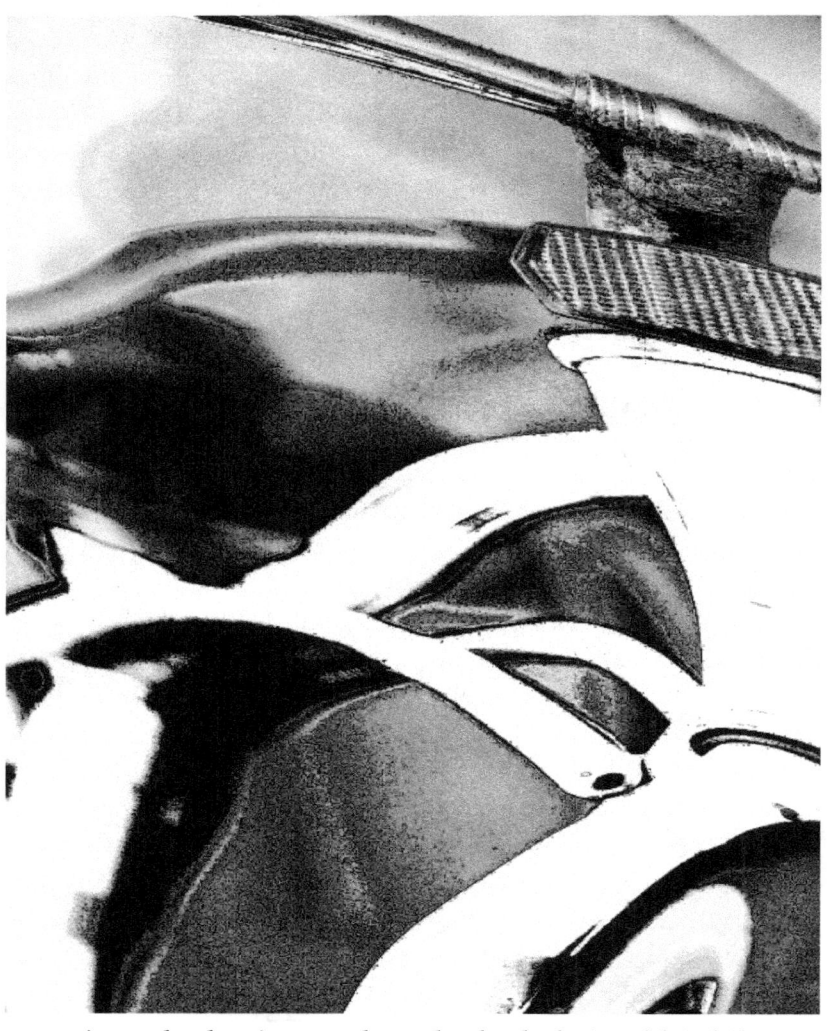

LATE AFTERNOON I WALKED back to my apartment in Frogtown from a small coffeehouse on University Avenue. I like to study out. It's so boring to be cooped up all the time, and all I did was study. Taking on a full load of credits and a lifetime of debt tends to mean you study a lot.

After a block, I passed this guy chaining up his bicycle. A sort-of metallic green Cannondale mountain bike. It looked new. As I passed by not thinking about anything, I saw him struggle to put his Kryptonite lock around a signpost and lock it. Strange how it caught my eye: he set the bar into the U part and turned the key, but, as he got up, he left his keys hanging off the side. I kept walking, of course, but it stuck in my mind. A half a block away, I stopped and looked back. The guy went into the business where he had chained his bike.

I pulled my backpack off, set it on the ground and leaned against the building. I stood there for a good five, ten minutes, considering something I never considered considering. Should I take it?

It's not in my nature to take things that don't belong to me. Did I need a bicycle? Not really. I had one at home. Then why take it? But I wanted it. It would be easy. There were a fair number of people walking around, doing their business, all potential witnesses, but I figured that no one would know that it wasn't my sort-of metallic green Cannondale mountain bike if I sauntered over, unlocked the Kryptonite and peddled off. My heart pumped and I was getting high on adrenaline even though I hadn't done anything yet. I liked it. The perfect antidote to reading the Myth of Sisyphus for the last two hours.

BILL BURLESON is the author of numerous works of fiction including *Hunting in the Dark* (Bartleby-Snopes 2014) and *Bi-America* (Rutledge 2005). He lives in Minneapolis.

Finally, feeling stupid for standing there so long, I slung my backpack on my shoulder and walked back. I tried to move slowly so as not to draw suspicion and kept telling myself to act naturally. Just another college student on a bicycle. I got to the sort-of metallic green Cannondale mountain bike and stopped. I felt like I had drunk a hundred cups of coffee. A thin young woman with long blond hair walked by and I said hello. She ignored me. I looked around, all nonchalant, then bent down, turned the key and released the lock. For some reason I took the time to reassemble the lock and put it in its spot on the frame, as if it mattered. I should have just dropped it on the ground.

"Hey, Justin, someone's stealing your bike!"

I almost shit myself. Some guy came out of the storefront that the bicycle guy had entered. It struck me as surreal, both the situation of me getting caught stealing a bicycle and the fact that he was barefoot and wearing a white Karate uniform complete with black belt.

Instead of wisely running away, I swung the sort-of metallic green Cannondale mountain bike up over my head and started running down the street.

After a quarter block, I looked back and saw a seemingly endless stream of white guys coming out of the business, all wearing Karate uniforms and pointing at me. I guess it was a Dojo. Who knew? The students started running after me and were gaining fast as I ran down the street with the bicycle over my head.

The fastest among them had almost caught up to me, now a good block away from the scene of the crime, when it dawned on me that bicycles have wheels for a reason. I dropped the sort-of metallic green Cannondale mountain bike down and got on as fast as I could, not one second too soon. After gaining some headway, I maneuvered off the sidewalk and into the street, peddling like a maniac. After about a block, I looked back. What a sight: there must have been twenty or so Karate students chasing me, and they weren't giving up.

Looking over my shoulder, I didn't see the Cadillac Escalade stopped at a light. I slammed into the back and fell to the ground in a heap. Stunned, I laid there for a second or two, not knowing what happened.

I came to my senses with this big black guy with gold teeth and a Devil Rays jacket leaning over me.

"What the fuck! You broke my window! Stupid punk, look at this shit!"

I got up, head hurting. The back window safety glass spider webbed where my head hit. I picked up the sort-of metallic green Cannondale mountain bike. It looked OK.

"Who cares about your bike? Look at the window, not to mention the scratches! You better have some insurance, boy." Three other huge black guys came out of the Cadillac to survey the damage.

Even though it seemed like a day had passed since I took the sort-of metallic green Cannondale mountain bike, it must have been less than a minute. I looked back to see the Karate students still coming down the street, hauling ass and looking for blood. I looked down and saw my backpack had split open and the contents were all over the ground. What's two-hundred dollars in textbooks when your hide is at stake? I jumped on the bike and started peddling on down the street. "Bitch! Get back here!" the man with gold teeth yelled. But I was gone, standing on the pedals and hauling ass.

I looked back. The three Cadillac passengers ran after me, adding to the twenty or so Karate dudes, barefoot wearing GI's, about a half block behind. I had speed on my side. But not for long. I glanced back to see the Karate students part like the Red Sea for the big Cadillac Escalade.

I took a right turn into a parking lot. By the time I crossed the lot, the Cadillac was gaining fast with the barefoot black belts trailing behind. I had to lose them, so, putting the mountain bike's knobby tires to use, I whizzed like a lunatic through a backyard and then between two old brownstones too close together for the Escalade to follow.

I popped out from between the buildings and onto the front lawn and a child's birthday party, complete with balloons, streamers and an army of children. Trying to dodge the little five-year-olds, I smashed right into a grill full of ribs and, my body now airborne, onto the food table. Beans and rice, tortillas and barbequed chicken flew everywhere.

A cake at the end of the table flipped up in the air and landed in the face of this huge guy I think was the father. Like some sort of urban Three Stooges, there he stood wearing a muscle shirt, neck tattoo and marble cake.

The children screamed. The apparent mother yelled at me in Spanish. The big guy just stood there. Six other guys, with dates and wives and beer bottles and muscle shirts of their own, stared at me. Then the father. Then me. I slid off the picnic table. The plump little mother added to her yelling "¡Usted monstruo! ¡Usted diablo!" by slapping at me. I picked up the sort-of metallic green Cannondale mountain bike, bowed and apologized while getting slapped all the way into the street. The father stood in the same place now pulling cake off his head as the six other guys started talking to each other and pointing. Right then, the twenty or so white students and the three huge black passengers from the Cadillac ran right into the party.

I jumped on and rode like hell. I got half a block when up ahead the Cadillac Escalade rounded the corner, coming right at me. I looked back to see the Karate students, three Cadillac passengers and now six muscle shirt guys all giving chase. I took a left into a parking lot, packed with cars. Getting up some steam, I peddled across the block and through the driveway alongside what appeared to be a funeral home. Looking back, I didn't see the Cadillac, but the rest of the city was still back there, including the mother, bringing up the rear, arms flailing, slapping me in absentia.

I got to the front of the building and found myself in a crowd of Hmong people. I skidded to a stop, and this time I didn't hit anyone. I hopped off and started picking my way through the throng of people, all looking at me like I'm nuts. "Sorry, sorry. Excuse me. Sorry."

I got to the street and hopped back on the sort-of metallic green Cannondale mountain bike. Cars were parked everywhere, leaving no driving lane. I saw over the car roofs the Cadillac come around the corner to the west, so I went east. The Cadillac couldn't get anywhere as I zipped and swerved between the mourner's cars.

I almost made it to the end of the block, when a Hmong guy stepped out of the side of a van right into my path. With little room to maneuver, I hit him square on. We both landed on our asses. A rooster squawked and flew up in the air. As I lay on the ground, the red rooster standing on a car hood, it occurred to me that maybe this was a dream, and maybe I should stay here, on my back, on the asphalt. As I stared into the sky, a group of teen boys in suits showed up, yelling stuff about what the hell was I doing, dude, you're in trouble now, etcetera. I got up. I grabbed the Sort-of metallic green Cannondale mountain bike and noticed the chain had come off. I held it over my head and ran. The teens gave chase, catching up almost immediately, just as the Cadillac did, having had time to go around the block, appeared in front of us. Meanwhile, the mob finally caught up and surrounded me. I stood there, sort-of metallic green Cannondale mountain bike overhead, greasy chain now hanging in my face, circled by the twenty or so white Karate students, three huge black passengers from the Cadillac, six tattooed Latino guys in the muscle shirts, about eight or ten teen Hmong funeral goers and a rooster on a car hood. Everything fell strangely quiet. I broke the silence:

"Can't we all just get along?"

The first person to hit me was the mother, who ran through the crowd yelling "¡Voy a matarle! ¡Voy a matarle!" slapping in the air until she was slapping me.

Right as the crowd began to join in, me defenseless with the bicycle still above my head, a Latina woman ran up the street yelling, "¡El edificio por fuego! ¡El edificio por fuego!" The men in the muscle shirts turned and frantically pushed their way back through the pack.

Everyone else stopped, understanding something bad was happening, even if they didn't understand what the woman had said. In about a second, the problem was obvious as a big cloud of smoke drifted around us. The twenty or so white Karate students, three huge black passengers from the Cadillac plus the driver and about eight or ten teen Hmong funeral goers took off following the muscle shirt guys.

I stood there for an eternity, at first stunned, then wondering what was up with the rooster still standing on the car hood, and then weighing my options. After about two seconds of this eternity, I ran like Adrian Peterson the other direction.

That night, I found out on the news that a fire started when coals from the grill I wiped-out got on a tablecloth catching it afire, making the picnic table catch, blowing embers in a window, igniting the drapes and there ya go.

The twenty or so white Karate students, three huge black passengers from the Cadillac plus the driver and about eight or ten teen Hmong funeral goers worked together going door to door and warning everyone to get out.

Meanwhile, the muscle shirt guys got their car fire extinguishers and put out the fire.

They were all hailed as heroes, as saving the neighborhood.

And that's how the Frogtown Multicultural Fair started. Ever since that day, there has been a street fair in front of the funeral home marking the occasion when the neighborhood got together and fought the fire. There are bike races, Karate demonstrations, barbequed chicken and red beans and rice.

Happily, the authorities never came knocking. Plus, I had a new bicycle.

The bad news? From then on, I had to bike somewhere far away to study and drink coffee.

Haiku & Close To
Steven Schild

Eros in Autumn

Eros in autumn:
Old men admire young women
for what they once were.

Cruel Eyes Don't Look

Cruel eyes don't look
at older women passing
for what they once were.

Nothing Matters More

Nothing matters more
than love, or so we say when
sunny is the day.

But when pain courses
blood-thick through our veins, will our
bright resolve remain?

STEVE SCHILD is the author of *Eros in Autumn* (Up On Big Rock Poetry Series 2014). He lives and teaches in Winona.

Love Song: A Lamentation

Birds do not sing
to the wings that bear them
or eagles to the air
that carries them
to places they did not know
they could go.
Lungs hum no lyrics
to the ether that fills them,
nor do hearts drum hymns
to the blood that wills them
almost endlessly on.

And I do not sing
to what I every day see,
which makes it so clear,
my dearest of dears,
that it is oh, so wrong,
that for oh, so long,
you have heard no love song
from me.

Old Men outside the Library

Chalky bones challenge
steep marble steps, so moved by
the smell of old books.

After All That

Crow, on a tombstone,
takes a shit; after all that
life comes down to this.

Children

Like crystal they glow
and may shatter so, thus this
cruel truth we know:

Love's never enough.

The Way I Want to Go

May my heart explode
with me in full stride chasing
what I hope to catch.

LENOI
Emilio DeGrazia

A mind poet
Stays in the house.
The house is empty
And it has no walls.
The poem
Is seen from all sides,
Everywhere,
At once.
Gary Snyder, *As for Poets*

I DON'T KNOW WHAT POSSESSED ME to detour onto the township road. Maybe I needed to return to a place I'd been to but never seen. So I found myself mainly lost on a road in the northern Minnesota county where my ancestors had settled when the European immigrant waves hit the north shore of Lake Superior in the 1880's. I'd driven through the North Shore area as a tourist, but never as soloist playing out a nostalgia as full of longing as it was empty of usefulness. I was bored, yes, but also divorced from a second wife and from most things new and in the news. I needed to start over again, return to some starting point, this time on a township road leading I knew not where.

The sign appeared about a hundred yards past an abandoned farmhouse so broken and worn it reminded me of my mother in the last month of her life. No doubt, the house had been formidable in its day. Its three levels rose above a sagging porch to the attic gable crowning its façade, and from the fascia boards' gingerbread trim was hanging down like icicles. My mother would have been at home in the place. I had her in view as I drove past and almost could see her on the porch: Strong woman lording it over her family a hundred years ago, dame who needed only a hard stare to get her way. As I drove past the façade of the house turned toward me, and because I glanced back I almost missed the sign: GORDIE'S ANTIQUES. NEXT LEFT. With dull blue letters hand-painted on plywood, the sign was nailed to the trunk of a fat oak run through by barbed wire that fenced out the township road. A blackbird, perhed on a strand of the wire, turned its head to eye me as I drove past. It seemed strange standing there alone, the rainbow colors on its back disappearing as the sun ducked behind a mass of clouds.

EMILIO DEGRAZIA, emeritus professor at Winona State University, is the author of many books. In 2013-2014, he served as Poet Laureate in Winona, where he resides.

The way to Gordie's was a gravel path that crossed a culvert as it wound its way up an incline overlooking the township road. There, almost hidden from view by a jungle of bushes and trees, stood an old barn long winters had stripped bare of paint. The yard was a mazework of things, junk crowding in on itself—wagon wheels, bales of wire, chunks of broken farm machinery, harnesses, tin buckets, and, standing at attention next to the front door, a Mobile Oil gasoline pump with its hose hanging to one side like a dead arm. A collector's paradise, I smirked as I tried the door.

"Hello." The word wound its way into a dusty silence as dim as the light in the place. The old barn was dense with stuff, junk piled on junk, more stuff on display cases and chairs, bookcases jammed with dishes and cups, pictures and frames hanging from nails, all of it dusted by the odor of old age. I tried again: "Anybody home?" Again, my words disappeared into the spaces between things, crevices too small to let light in or out.

I began meandering through the narrow aisles, not looking for any one thing. Rather immediately, I felt as if I were being watched, not by a person but by the things in the place. And as my eyes wandered aimlessly, I developed a strange sense that one particular thing—I didn't know what was following my moves.

"Anybody home?" I said again with a voice that whistled in the dark.

"What are *you* doing here?"

The words were pointed and blunt. They targeted *me*. I looked around.

"You're just looking. I know what you're doing. You don't know what you're looking for."

The voice came from the wall behind me, above my left shoulder. As I turned, I saw the jar––facing me, sitting alone atop an old mahogany dresser missing a middle drawer. It was rough, dark and round, its surface and rim dulled by wear, its torso evoking the breasts, belly and thighs of a well-rounded woman, headless.

"You don't know what you want."

For a moment, I was caught between the two, the invisible voice and the jar eyelessly facing me. I turned in time to glimpse a movement in the portrait of a patriarch hanging on the chimney wall. The face in the portrait, austere and gray against a background of black, blinked as it moved to one side, leaving me with nothing but an empty frame.

"I know your type," he said as he peered down from behind the showcase close to the chimney wall. "You're wasting your time, and mine."

The thin strands of his hair fell carelessly down on all sides, and his face had an ashen hue. He seemed ordinary in his flannel shirt and overalls, old and frail enough to pose no threat except through eyes that seemed uncannily blue. The nastiness of his tone challenged me, even as the jar stood behind me impassively.

"I am looking, sir, maybe with a mind to buy."

"No, you won't really buy."

I reeled, my mind wholly made up. "I want *that.*"

"The jar?"

"Yes, *it.*"

"No, you don't want *that.*"

"It's for sale. This is Gordie's Antiques. Things here are for sale, aren't they? I want to buy that urn."

"No, it costs too much."

"What's your price?"

"Too much. It's old."

"How old?"

"Old."

"Is it dated?"

"Real old. Not sure how old. That's your business, not mine."

I leaned down close, looking for a price tag.

"It's cracked," the old man said, "on the inside."

"How much?"

"It's cracked—on the inside."

He glared at me as I picked it up. The thing immediately conformed itself to my hold, its contours so smooth it seemed that the jar's gravity had been transformed into buoyancy in my hands.

"I'll buy it."

He looked away.

"How much you asking?"

"Three-ninety."

Three hundred and ninety dollars? The old man was dead-set on provoking a fight. As he stepped into the aisle, he fumbled in the pocket of his overalls. He came out with a dime.

"No tax. I don't believe in tax," he said. "You got four ones?"

I handed four one-dollar bills into a quivering hand.

"I'm curious about this vase," I said. "When it dates from. Where it came from."

"Came from the house just up the road. Nostrum house."

"Nostrum? I'm a Nordstrom. Close enough. Barry Nordstrom's my name."

"Old lady lived there alone. Nobody there now. Everybody dead and gone."

"Where'd they come from?"

"Don't know."

"Well Gordie," I said, "thank you."

"I'm not Gordie. That's just a name, a sign," he said as he turned away and faded into the mazework of things. "I'm somebody else."

***

I cradled the jar in my arms as I left, feeling like a thief and a fool. At $3.90, the jar was a steal. Certainly, he could have commanded a heftier price, especially after triggering my passion to buy. But the jar was not a flower vase and no Grecian urn, and I had half a mind to damn the impulse that surrendered to the jar's allure. Was it destined to spend a few weeks on a table or shelf before becoming just another thing that gets in the way? The $3.90 took up much less space than the jar, so maybe the joke was on me. Maybe the thing now owned me. Still I kept running my hands over it as I walked to the car, groping its curves like a blind man trying to find his way.

I wrapped it in a towel and propped it on the front seat of the car. We would have to drive carefully all the way home, avoid bumps and sudden stops. I imagined where I could keep her in the house—the dining room table, the bookcase in the living room, the mantle above the fireplace, or the walnut shelf facing the portrait of gloom and doom-faced Grandfather Nordstrom, who never took his unforgiving eyes off the portrait of my mother hanging above the dining room table. "How about the walnut shelf?" I said. In her blanket of silence, the jar kept her opinions to herself as we floated non-stop through the two hundred mile trip back to my front door in St. Paul.

You may think I'm crazy to talk to a thing. But pause a moment to listen to yourself. We all carry on conversations with our pets—dogs, for example, canaries and cats, all of them capable of noising a response. But don't we also jabber at creatures that just stare at us—hamsters, goldfish and pet snakes? And who hasn't cursed a stone or rug for getting in the way of clumsy feet? Then name one person who hasn't stared at a clock and actually spoken to it, told it to slow down, mind its own business, tell the truth.

By the time I got the jar home I had decided on the fireplace mantle. As I set it there I decided it looked good, its rough curves smoothed out in the dim light. But as soon as I stepped back I sensed that it was training its attention on me when I turned my back. That first night I lay wide-eyed in bed as if I couldn't get the dripping of a faucet out of my head, thinking there's a reason she wants me awake, something she wants me to know. This jar was no figure or face casually passed on the street, the one who catches your eye, maybe almost flirts before moving on like an opportunity you'll never see again. The jar seemed to know something about me, and I knew nothing about it. Some meaning, as readable as the ink and paper of a message in a bottle washed ashore in a distant sea, was figured in its headless form.

As the weeks passed and the winter snows arrived the ghost jar in my house closed me in too. The jar haunted me. I unplugged the TV and stored up enough wood to keep the fireplace alive every night, and I must confess, Dear Reader, that I don't really believe in ghosts. But the jar, especially when night was silenced by deep snows outside, had a presence as real as any white-sheeted vapor conjured by superstitious minds. Above the blaze in the fireplace, the jar stared through walls at me, eyelessly. It was the center of gravity in the house, the focal point toward which other objects—the blank TV screen, the family photos hanging on walls, the antique grandfather's clock I had picked up at an estate sale for a song—directed their gaze. I admit to having had urges to be rid of the thing, throw it in a landfill and be done with it. But there too I see it rising above the fate thrust on it: Enthroned atop a huge mound of garbage and junk, its queenly form conspicuous against a background of trees and sky.

One sleepless night—the old clock had just tolled four a.m.—I took the jar in my hands. I was careful and gentle with it. I actually caressed the thing, recognizing what I often forget, that it's one thing to float loosely through surroundings as a free agent ignorant of the pavement, the traffic of people and cars, the grass and trees, even the air we breathe, all of them ordinarily unfelt as shapes, presences and powers. But it's something else to feel the reality of an object firmly established in the world of facts outside the mind. With the jar in my hands I was no longer an isolated and disconnected free-floating self. Its form fit me, its energy humming faintly into my fingers as I ran them over the jar's rough surfaces. I touched the jar in the way I had never touched a woman before.

Right then I wanted the jar to have a name, and I could have given her one—Maria came to mind, then Lydia—but I could not imagine her not already having been named. I wanted to know that name—and her place, where she was from. I brought her to the light and turned her slowly, re-examining the surface and underside for any sign of a signature. Then I brought her close to listen to her, the snow outside silencing the house enough for me to hear in its hollow the seasurf that becomes audible when we cup a seashell to an ear. Gordie who was not Gordie had mentioned a crack, so I went looking for it in the jar's dark well. In there I could not see to see. I grabbed a flashlight and aimed the beam into the jar, circling as I scoped. What took me as I gazed was a spiraling that seemed to rise as its ridges descended into the jar's well, the work of fingers that once upon a time had carefully circled toward the jar's depths in moist clay. I saw no crack. The jar was a marvel, its inner beauty invisible to the naked eye.

More than ever, I required the jar's truth. Who to ask, how learn more about this strange and wonderful thing? I brought it in close again and took a deep whiff. The room was in it, the odor of embers slowly dying in the fireplace, and, to be sure, a musky human scent, faintly of urine. Or was I wrong? Was I finding myself in it? Quite by accident my index finger found a scratch just inside the lip. Was this the crack the old man had warned me about, the jar's defect?

I circled the jar's rim, feeling nothing the first

time around. Then I softened the pressure, and there, just below the rim, I felt again the faint scar etched into the clay. My fingers felt their way over the hieroglyph, but they did not know how to read a surface as strange and subtle as this. I lay the jar on its side and brought the flashlight in close again.

The letters were small, no more than a quarter-inch tall, and they had been inscribed at an angle almost completely out of view. One by one I made the figures out and added them up: "LENOI."

LENOI. Somebody's—the potter's—name?

***

It was bitterly cold the next morning, the snow a foot deep on the lawns. I shoveled a path from the garage to the street, then went back in for the jar. I wrapped it carefully in a sheet and snuggled it next to me on the seat, my breath frosting the windshield as I tried the key. The car burped, sputtered and whined. Nothing. I waited, my breath thickening on the glass. More whining, dulling as it died. At that moment, I had the urge to call my mother. She would hustle me back into the house, warm my hands, put hot soup in front of me. But I couldn't remember what number to call, couldn't see she had died years ago. "Damn you!" I yelled at the car, and went inside to warm myself.

When I came back out, I popped the car's hood and pushed the spark plug wires down tight. I tried the ignition again, and again the engine burped, sputtered and whined. "God damn you!" I screamed, just as the engine coughed and fired.

The traffic was light when I reached downtown, and the plows had piled snow high on the curbs. I circled the Historical Museum three times before finding a space several blocks away. I squeezed the car in, gathered the jar in my arms, locked the car doors, and walked toward the Museum.

The curator's receptionist assured me no one knew more about old jars. "So if he clams up and gets a weird look on his face," she laughed, "it's because he's interested in it."

As I unraveled the sheet and placed the jar on the curator's desk, he stood apart as if bored. For a long moment he stared at the jar, then zeroed in, donning strange spectacles rigged with a lamp device of the sort doctors wear when performing surgery. He asked permission to pick it up, then weighed it in his hands, slowly feeling his way around the jar's curves.

"On the inside rim," I offered, "I think the word is LENOI."

"Obviously."

"The potter's name?"

"No, not a name. The potters left no names. Ghost hands worked their pots."

"But if it's not the potter's name?"

"*Le Noi.* All of us. *Ours.*"

"Ours?"

"*Ours.*"

"What does that mean?"

He shrugged. "*Ours.*"

"How old?"

He held it to the light again. "Dark red ochre. Southern France, Languedoc. But too old to be a Cathar piece. Maybe really old, before the time of Christ."

"Cathar?"

"Cathars. Twelfth century Christian heretics. Pope Innocent the Third felt obliged to kill them all. Called them the 'Church of Satan.' They had cults, you know, and in some of the cults women ran the show."

He turned the jar in his hands, almost lovingly, then lifted it and did a strange thing: He sniffed its insides. In the slight trembling of his hands, I saw the passion my jar inspired in him.

"You want to make a gift of it to the Museum?"

"*Give* it away?"

"You would realize a significant tax benefit."

Three dollars and ninety cents.

"I'd need to study it more, do some carbon dating, *et cetera*, but I'm confident we could make you an offer for it. The piece is several hundred years old, maybe more. It could be a rare example of pre-Christian art from the area. You should let us purchase the piece. She belongs in the public domain, and she would make you a pretty wad of cash."

"I think not," I said as I took her from him. "But can you tell me one more thing? What did they do with her in ancient times? What did they put in her?"

"Wine, water, oil, seeds. Barley," he said as he looked at me with new hope in his eyes. "You don't use barley, do you? You'd never think to put barley in her. Or olive oil. And it's cracked. Are you sure you won't sell? Give it some thought."

***

I was not sure of anything. Again, the car wouldn't start and I spent half a day waiting for a mechanic to arrive. We ended up towing the thing through two miles of city streets to his garage. Two more hours passed before the mechanic delivered his bottom line: The car, no offense please, was a piece of junk and I should get rid of it, and that's why he would only charge me $175 for the repairs. I drove it home, leaving it idling on the street as I shoveled a new pathway for it to the garage, all the time wondering how much the jar might fetch from the weird man in the Museum.

That night the jar's presence filled the room. The thing's headlessness, atop a form so obviously shaped as breasts, belly and thighs, made it an alien. Where a face should have been there was an abstracted absence that kept taking different shapes on the grainy wallpaper above the fireplace. I kept turning away from its eyeless stare, twisting and turning my view of her: Did its round form add up not to a body but also a head––temple, eyebrows, cheekbones, mouth and receding chin? Was its form a face? Yes, I said as I screwed and unscrewed my eyes, but no. Don't make of things what they are not, I told myself as the jar stared at me.

I did not know what I did not know, but I knew what I had to do. "No," I said aloud, "you're not coming along. You stay home where you belong. I don't trust that car with you in it."

The next morning the car started right up and I found myself under a frigid blue sky heading for the North Shore and my township road. Don't ask me to explain all the reasons why. The jar had a story for me, and I'd never get to it by taking straight logical steps. I drove recklessly toward the only source I knew, with clouds low in the sky by the time I drove past the sign for Gordie's Antiques. Snow was drifting down as I stood staring at the handwritten note on Gordie's door: CLOSED.

The man in Gordie's had no name, so for my impractical purposes he didn't exist. I backtracked to the car and eased myself onto the township road. I turned left, knowing I had another option open to me, even as the wind picked up and snow began dimming the late afternoon sun.

I parked the car just off the township road and trudged to the broken farmhouse I had glimpsed while speeding past some months earlier. My mother had died on a hot sunny day, and the abandoned house, when I stared at it, gave me the sense of dread I felt when I saw her laid out in the casket for the first time. The house seemed pallid, its weather beaten siding whitened by the snow blanketing the field that stretched out before the two front windows gazing blankly down as I approached. No light on anywhere in the house. No smoke rising from the chimney. No heat. Nobody home.

I felt suddenly free as I locked in my resolve. It was absurd, it was illegal—breaking and entering——but once it became a done deal in my mind the careful person I knew myself to be lost himself in the strange obsession that had brought him here. The façade of the house had a flat expression, and one of its bedroom wings had sunk far enough into the ground to reveal a gaping roofline crack. I tried a few windows and then the cellar door before I tried the obvious. The front door was unlocked.

Empty and cold. The living room, the dining room, the bedrooms downstairs. Barren to the walls, except for a grand piano, covered by a sheet, staring in silence out a bay window at a field full of dry weeds. On the kitchen table, I found a candle and box of matches left behind by some other visitor, one of those small strokes of chance that make or break a fate. I lit a match, seeing the small flash as a stranger would see a headlight in a mirror while speeding by on the township road. I held it to the candle wick. The candle flared before it settled into a steady glow. Let there be light.

The trap door to the attic challenged me. Twice I lost my balance on the narrow steps as I pushed on the small door outlined in cedar trim. I slammed against it with my open hand, worried that the sound would waken everyone for miles around. Finally, with one last push and fistful slam, its edges cracked and I had an opening. I don't know what rained on me then—dust and dirt and bat guano and more dust that decades had turned into bad air. A frigid draft yawned in the darkness above me like one of the cold circles of Dante's hell.

The candle went out as I found my footing on rafters supporting the trap door. For a long moment, I was hopelessly lost in the dark, balancing there like a giant vulture on splayed legs. I sat in the dark, then resolved to enter it. As I inched forward on the rafters supporting the attic roof I began feeling my way past a chimney wall, and as I turned a corner a beam of moonlight showed me the way.

There, beneath the small gable window I found the old hatbox under a newspaper that had been sucked by a draft into the space where the roof meets the front wall. The only other visible thing was a bat, either asleep or dead, clinging to a roof beam. The hatbox was stuffed full of papers, letters, old documents. I tucked the hatbox under my arm and did my tightrope walk across the rafters, squeezed myself through the trap door, and made my way down the stairs.

I locked the hatbox in the trunk after the car again refused to start. I finally flagged down a stranger willing to haul me to a mechanic willing to tow the car to town. "Oh we'll fix you up alright," the mechanic said, "so you can be on your way. We'll have it good as new."

But I knew better than to believe in him. Both my divorces had left me feeling like a car that refused to start in the cold.

***

In the quiet isolation of my house, my family history stared at me. On the living room wall, portraits of Grandmother and Grandfather Nordstrom faced each other with blonde frowns, while my father, young man with hat in hand, stood next to a suitcase smiling at the camera. There I was too, cocky college graduate looking down at the world, my older sister too young to strike false poses in her First Communion dress. My two ex-wives were there too, snapshots taken in happier times, both of them perky and small in their plain wooden frames, and avoiding eye contact with everyone in the room. Some day, I kept thinking, I would give everyone a new place in the house, then begin the task of rearranging all my books, organizing them on shelves from the first-read to the last. If I got the time-line right, together they might tell a tale. My mother's portrait above the dining room table said no, look at me, don't keep looking the other way, while the jar, back in its place above the fireplace, seemed satisfied and calm, at home.

I spread the hatbox contents on the table and moved a light in close. "Well, then, here we are," I said, gazing up at the jar dancing in place above the nice blaze I had started in the fireplace.

I'm not sure why a stash of old papers left behind by people long gone draws us in. Liver-spotted pages feel too tender to the touch, as if the dim and carefully crafted handwriting seems not only foreign but doomed to disintegrate before anyone can make sense of it. If we all need to script our own story, if only in our own minds, then antique papers may take us just far enough back to give us the chance to begin in the middle of things in that long time before we were born. We're still far from centered there, but we're present enough to try making sense of things by going forward and back. And when we give ourselves long enough pause we keep going back and back beyond any shadow of the former self we still recognize ourselves to be—toward ancestors who seem more and more like aliens as we discover they are blood-kin.

I know that now, because I stole the hatbox from the old house.

In all the musty books, libraries and museums I've visited all I've ever found is a stray clue here or there. These clues lurk like snakes underground in the dark ages where we mainly live.

I spent the whole night studying each bill of sale, every receipt, newspaper clipping and property deed the hatbox spilled into my hands. There were nine letters too, and I stayed with them until I made out every word. When finally I lay my head down on a pillow the sun was already halfway up in the morning sky, bright enough for me to close my eyes in full confidence that in the papers I had stolen I had nothing certain at all.

Four hours later, I awoke with a start, full of a curiosity for things I could not locate in memory or dream. I went over the letters again, trying to stretch a few fragments into a coherent history.

…Catharine Nostrum of Montpelier in France….never wanted to come to America….

Catharine. Where did this name come from?

…sent Agnes and George a special vase as a wedding gift….
…Catharine always said things…the vase was rare, sacred to an ancient cult….

A Cathar jar? Or more ancient pre-Christian pagan one?

…and then Agnes refused to take George's name! Think of that! Who did she think she was?
…he took a woman whenever he got drunk….

…and after George went out into the storm of 1889 to save his horse (God save us), Agnes knew he was gone for good….

…after her mother died in 1901….everything in the house was Laura's, the dishes, the old tables and chairs, the old vase George used as a pisspot next to his bed….
…Laura kept it all, that witch….

Who did she think she was? Then Laura died. And the auctioneer appeared. And the jar crowded its way into Gordie's Antiques. And here I was still in the dark, gazing out the window at the snow brilliant in the sunlight of a blue-skied afternoon. A story here, but no history. My jar a vessel sacred to an ancient cult, and George's pisspot too. Do we dare leap from Cathar to Catharine without passing through the dark ages separating LENOI from Nostrum? Both are *ours*. And now that the jar was mine, in my house, what invisible thread tied me to LENOI? Did Nostrum trek north to find a blonde blue-eyed Nordstrom mate, so that a filament as fine as a DNA strand made me a distant relative of LENOI? As I thought back and back I became a stranger to myself, weirdly both Adam and Eve, father and mother, brother and sister mating incestuously to bear new children and more absurdly yet a child of this mother-jar too, dark seed vessel from ancient times.

That day I walked the three miles to the cemetery, chilled to the bone as I passed through the gate. Only the brow of the stone over my mother's grave was visible in the deep snow.

On my knees I brushed away the snow with my hand until her name became visible on the small plaque. Why had I not brought flowers with me, at least one white rose? In the sub-zero air, its freshness would have frozen hard as glass until the spring rains fell. "I'm sorry, sorry, Mother," I said, "I missed you all those years." I cried and cried.

I shuddered in the cold as I walked back, seeing them clearly now, the beautiful women sitting at café tables in the summer sun, the slender one reading a book on the bus, the smart-aleck ones who never looked my way as they passed me on the sidewalks, and the old lady still on the other side of a street, the one a bit lost and confused, loaded down by grocery bags and the heaviness of her belly and thighs.

I was in no hurry to get home and shut myself inside. If by luck or chance, one of those women came my way I would smile and do my best to find words.

Black & White
Sally Niemand

SALLY NIEMAND loves finding beauty in her surroundings. At the age of 12, she got a Brownie camera. In 1975, she got her first *big girl* camera, a 35 mm SLR. A Midwest native, Sally lives in Orange Park, Florida.

Zen of Winter

A boy, a dog and a rock

Fantasia

Milwaukee Museum of Art

Inner Beauty

Shadow of a Doubt

Pemaquid Point Lighthouse, Maine

Over the Unknown: Three Poems
Andy Roberts

Counterclockwise

The lake small enough to throw a rock across
but the path that follows its banks takes me
all morning to wander. Trail blazed with
bright red cardinal flower, I meander
counterclockwise against the day's obligations,
my goal to explore the lakeshores, streambeds and riversides,
to say I love you to this country
in a poem without a false note.

The trail climbs over twisted roots of sycamores
one thousand years old, following the scissor
of their white legs into darkness,
counterclockwise against the new century's creep.
I was born one million years ago,
rising upright from all fours to pluck a berry,
build a pyramid, write a sonnet to another's eyes.
Where satellite reception fails honeysuckle fills my nose.

Resting on a fallen log, eyes closed,
two fingertips of my right hand against my left wrist,
the splash of bluegill jumping in shallow water
every thirty heartbeats.
A feast of midges swirling in columns
over green lotus, pink and yellow blooms.
Counterclockwise against insurance, knowing only
where the journey started, I rise.

Another goal is to wear out eighty five pairs of hiking boots,
one pair a year: a substantial body of work.
Then use them as a funeral pyre,
the stench of burning vibram repelling any mourners.
My journey more than halfway done.
The sun, through treetops, straight overhead.
The path I follow circular, counterclockwise to the start.
My heart continuous, until it stops.

ANDY ROBERTS' poetry has appeared in many
journals including *Atlanta Review* and *Meridian
Anthology of Contemporary Poetry*. His latest
collection is *The Green World* (Night Ballet
Press, 2014). Andy lives in Columbus, Ohio.

Four O'clock in the Afternoon

Looking north through open blinds of rain splattered window,
early April lawn just turning green.
Coldest winter in living memory
slowly giving up the ghost.
Cloud rags running east
over tree line – ash, maple, oak.
Southern Ohio at four o'clock in the afternoon.
How I arrived
at this window
on a wet April afternoon
in early 21st century Ohio
makes no sense trying to explain.
But here I am with my green houseplants crawling toward light,
acoustic guitar on its stand,
leather couch, books on coffee table,
cherry wood mantle over fireplace with clock in center,
bifocals perched on my nose.
Fifty seven years to get here.
This mild rain. This ordinary life.
A starling stopped on a stem of staggergrass.
I watch him
shake the rain from his feathers,
spring forward into a lowering sky.
Neither of us knows where
we're going, but the starling,
busy being a bird, doesn't
care what time it is.

Seizure Creek

Suspension bridge over Caesar Creek washed out.
My wife, in her non-native English,
pronouncing it Seizure Creek.
We stare across the torrent
as we bite into hard Granny Smith apples.
Eight hundred years ago
a branch of the Shawnee stopped here,
called it home.
We look for traces of mounds
meant to guide the dead.

Descended from a line of Pennsylvania Quakers
convinced they would rest in heaven,
a sixty-two year old white man
built the first log cabin on Caesar Creek
two hundred years ago.
I throw my apple core in the river,
watch it float downstream.
Three miles back to the car
thinking of the faith it took
to shape serpent mounds,
suspend a bridge over the unknown.

Two Very Short Plays
Brandt Roberts

1. Oblivion

Characters in order of appearance:

Father/Grandfather

Daughter/Mother

Boyfriend/ Fiancé

Granddaughter

Moving man—1

Moving man—2

Note: The entire play is silent save for the TV and the Moving men.

Just a change in body language and stance is all that is required to illustrate the passage of time. There is a quick blackout between each scene: similar to the blip between changing a channel on a television. Some roles may be doubled.

BRANDT ROBERTS, a seasonal actor at the Lanesboro Commonweal Theater in 2014, appeared in *Arsenic and Old Lace* and *Arcadia*. He enjoys writing and sculpture, and lives in Kennett, Missouri.

Setting: A living room.

Scene 1

The Scene opens with the image of a recliner and an old television on the floor facing it. There is a small table next to the recliner. It holds a sub sandwich, a canned soft drink, and a TV Guide.

*The **father** is lounging in the recliner.*

Periodically he takes a bite of his sandwich and sips his soda. Static from the TV is projected onto his face. Every now and then, he changes the channel. However, the channels are always STATIC.

*The **daughter** is seated on the floor playing with a doll. She is about five years old. Eventually, she holds her doll up to the **father** in an effort to get him to play. The **father** aggressively motions the doll away, not wanting to miss a moment of television. The **daughter** retreats to a corner and hugs her doll. The **father** switches the channel.*

Scene 2

*It's the same setting. However, now the **daughter** is around ten. She is sitting reading a book. After a while, the **daughter** approaches her **father** and requests him to read. The **father** motions that he is eating and pushes the book away. The **daughter** reads alone. The **father** takes a bite of his sub and switches the channel.*

Scene 3

*The **daughter** is now a young woman (around sixteen). The **father** is watching a football game. Pep band music can be heard. The **daughter** is practicing a cheer for her cheerleading squad (although not heard). She is dancing and leaping about: full of life and energy. She leaps between her father and the TV. The **father** motions at her to move. The **daughter** draws back to another corner. The **boyfriend** enters. As soon as the **daughter** sees him, she bounds into his arms and gives him a kiss. They leave the stage arm in arm.*

*The **father** sips his soda and takes a bite of his sandwich. He browses through the TV guide for quite a while. Eventually, he finds something of interest and changes the channel.*

Scene 4

*The **daughter** is now a young lady. The **boyfriend** enters. Apparently, they are going on a date.*

*The **daughter** hugs him and gives him a peck on the cheek. The **boyfriend** drops down on one knee, takes a box out of his pocket and opens it. It's a ring. The girl is on the verge of tears and nods. The two hug and kiss passionately. They leave the stage to start their life together. The **father** sips his soda and races through the channels.*

Scene 5

*There is a child on the floor. She is the **granddaughter**. She is playing with the same doll that the daughter had earlier. She raises it toward her grandfather. The **grandfather** does not react. The **granddaughter** continues to shake the doll in his face, but to no avail. The **grandfather** lethargically changes the channel.*

Scene 6

*The **granddaughter** is now ten. She is sitting reading the same book. Next to her, the **mother** sits. The **mother** is listening to her child read. The **grandfather** lies asleep in the chair. The **mother** notices that he's asleep. She approaches him, gives him a kiss on the forehead and switches off the television.*

Black Out
Long pause.

Scene 7

Voices are heard in the darkness.

Moving Man—1

Hey, I think this is the last room!

Moving Man—2

All right! All right! I'm a coming!

***Moving Man—1** turns on the lights in the living room.*

The chair is empty. The table is empty. The room is void of life.

***Moving Man—2** enters.*

Moving Man—1

I'll get the TV. *(Picks up the TV and carries it off stage)*

Moving Man—2

Fine by me. This table looks lighter anyway.

(Picks up the table and follows suit.) They both return and are about to move the recliner.

Suddenly, **Moving Man—1** *pauses.* Huh. Seventy-one years... *(He pets the recliner)*

Moving Man—2

Excuse me?

Moving Man—1

Oh, I was thinking... If this chair could talk, imagine the stories it would tell.

Moving Man—2 shakes his head at his partner and the two men exit with the chair.

The stage is bare.

Black Out

2. Their Diner

Characters
Cook
Waitress
Busboy
Obese Man
Dr. Gordon Elliot
Tall Man

Setting: A diner, the present.

The scene is set in a diner in St. Louis. There is a bar with a grill, waffle irons, etc. where the Cook lives. Scattered about are booths, tables and chairs, and at one end of the bar is a cash register. Upstage is a door leading to the restrooms and stage right is situated the main door to the establishment. A jukebox sits beside the door. Behind the bar, a door leads the storeroom. The Cook is busy behind the counter. An Obese Man sits at a booth reading the menu. He wears sweatpants, a T-shirt and suspenders. The Waitress and the Busboy are talking inaudibly.

Cook: *(Singing out of tune and in a high falsetto)* "Hello, I love you! Won't you tell me your name?"

The door opens and in limps an older gentleman in a tweed suit. The left side of his body appears inhibited. He speaks in a soft slurred murmur. In his right hand, he carries a satchel stuffed with papers. He is a stroke victim with a peaceful demeanor.

Waitress: Morning Dr. Elliot! I hope you are well.

Gordon: *(nods and mumbles)* I'm well.

Waitress: I'm glad to hear it! *(She helps him to his seat)* Will you have the usual? *(Dr. Elliot nods)* I see you brought your papers. Are you writing some more poetry? *(Dr. Elliot smiles and nods)* I'm sure it will be great.

Cook: "Hello, I love you! Won't you tell me your name?"

Gordon: *(Laughs)* I hope so. *(Takes out papers and begins to write)*

Waitress: I'll be back with your coffee.

Gordon: Thank you.

Cook: "Hello, I love you! Won't you tell me your name?"

Waitress: *(Turns to the Obese man)* Are you ready to order?

Obese Man: *(softly morose)* Yes. I'll have an iced tea and a waffle.

Waitress: Will that be all?

Obese Man: *(pause)* Yes. *(He picks up a newspaper and begins the crossword puzzle)*

Cook: "Hello, I love you! Won't you tell me your name?"

The waitress gives the cook the two orders. The door opens and in strides a Tall Man who sits at the bar. He is wearing shorts that accentuate his long legs. The Waitress walks over to the Busboy and gives him a peck on the cheek. He runs his fingers thru her hair.

Tall Man: Hey! Can I have some service?

Waitress: Oh! Yes. I'm sorry sir, what'll it be?

Tall Man: I'll have a steak-melt on sourdough with loaded hash browns and a Coke.

Waitress: Yes sir, I'll have that right out! *(Hands order to the Cook)*

Cook: "Hello, I love you! Won't you tell me your name?"

The Waitress picks up the Obese Man's tea and takes it to his booth.

Waitress: Here you go!

Obese Man: Thanks. *(He picks up the sugar dispenser and begins to pour.)*

The Waitress then takes Gordon's coffee to his table.

Waitress: Here's your coffee, Dr. Elliot.

Gordon: *(Smiles courteously)* Thank you.

Waitress: What have you got so far?

Gordon: A few lines. *(Hands her the paper)*

Waitress: "Oh Man in the Moon!

Wherefore dost thou mourn and moan?

Is it for mankind's scorn?

Oh Man in the Moon!

Dost thou not know?

Thou art a lamp unto our Darkness.

Oh Man in the Moon!

Hast thou heard from a wise old one?

Thy Light is a reflection of the Son."

Cook: "Hello, I love you! Won't you tell me your name?"

Gordon: Do you like?

Waitress: Yes. I like it very much…

Gordon: Then take it.

Waitress: Do you mean it? *(Gordon nods)*

She leaves his table clutching the sheet. The Busboy frowns.

Tall Man: Psst! Waitress. *(She comes over. The Tall Man whispers)* What's with the old man?

Waitress: Well, his name's Gordon Elliot. I think he was some sort of professor before he had a stroke.

Tall Man: Huh. Well that explains it. For a second, I thought he was retarded.

Waitress: I'm sorry?

Tall Man: Well, talks like an idiot, doesn't he? *(Laughs)*

Waitress: *(appalled)* I—I have to go. *(The Waitress keeps busy wiping down tables)*

Cook: "Hello, I love you! Won't you tell me your name?"

Tall Man: *(To the Cook)* Hey! Don't you know Happy Birthday or something?

The Cook continues about his task without a word.

Cook: "Hello, I love you! Won't you tell me your name?" Order up!

Tall Man: Phew! It's like a broken record in here!

The Waitress picks up Gordon's order and takes it to his table. It's an omelet and a salad.

Waitress: Here you are, sir.

Gordon: *(Smiles and nods)* Thank you.

Waitress: I hope what he said didn't bother you. *(Indicates Tall Man)*

Gordon: *(Shrugs)* It's trivial.

Waitress: So you're not mad?

Gordon: *(Smiles)* Life's too short.

Cook: "Hello, I love you! Won't you tell me your name?"

Gordon: Focus on what matters.

The Obese Man stops pouring and stirs his tea. After a sip, he goes back to his crossword.

Waitress: Thanks for the advice. *(She glances over at the Busboy)*

Cook: Order up!

The Waitress crosses over and picks up the Obese Man's waffle. While she crosses to his booth, the Busboy stops her.

Busboy: What did he give you? *(Glances at Gordon)*

Waitress: Just a poem. That's all.

Busboy: I don't like him giving you stuff.

Waitress: What's wrong? *(Pause)* It's just a poem. It wouldn't hurt you to write one once in a while! *Moves past him and brings the Obese Man his waffle.* Here you go. Enjoy your meal.

Obese Man: Thanks. *(Begins to pour maple syrup on the waffle until the thing is saturated)*

Waitress: If you need anything, let me know.

Obese Man: *(pause)* No thank you. That'll be all. *(Begins to eat)*

Cook: "Hello, I love you! Won't you tell me your name?" Order up!

The Waitress picks up the Tall Man's order and takes it too him.

Waitress: Here's your food. *(Turns to leave but the Tall Man stops her)*

Tall Man: Wait! Here! Take these quarters. *(Stuffs a handful of change into her palm)* Put them in the jukebox. Maybe it'll get that infernal tune out of his skull!

The Waitress goes over, puts all of the change into the machine and chooses several songs. "Hotel California" begins to play.

Cook: *(singing along)* "Welcome to the Hotel California!"

Tall Man: Thank goodness! *(Begins to eat)*

Cook: "Such a lovely place…"

Tall Man: "Such a lovely place…"

The Cook and the Tall Man sing, while the Busboy and the Waitress dance.

Gordon smiles and conducts with his pen. The Obese Man sits and scowls. The song ends.

Cook: "Hello, I love you! Won't you tell me your name?"

Tall Man: Ach! *(He throws his silverware into his plate and buries his head in his hands)*

Gordon: *(Laughs)* Ah, the familiar refrain.

The cook is tugging childishly on the Waitresses apron strings.

Cook: Yah! Yah!

Busboy: You leave her alone!

Cook: What? *(As he tugs)* I'm not doing anything!

Busboy: You heard me!

Cook: Whoa! Settle down there, stud! I was just kidding!

Busboy: Yeah, I bet you were!

Waitress: It's all right. No harm done.

Busboy: Not yet…

A cell phone rings. The Tall Man answers.

Tall Man: Yeah, what? No! You've got to be joking. Again? How much is this going to set us back? Half a day! You listen to me, Joe! We've got a little over two weeks until the deadline. I want the fifth story done today! *(Folds up the phone)* Shoot!

During the commotion, Gordon motions for the Busboy, whispers in his ear and gives him a scrap of paper. The Busboy smiles.

Cook: What is it?

Tall Man: Oh, a man fell again!

Cook: Oh, that's bad… That's bad! *(Beat)* How far did he fall?

Tall Man: About a story and a half. I bet I know who it was, the klutz. If I know him, he probably used a pair of jumper cables clamped to a girder as a safety harness!

Cook: Aren't you going to call to see how he is?

Tall Man: Nah! I don't want to hear it! It was a six-O-two, so he probably just sprained his ankle.

Cook: Oh. Well that's good.

The Busboy drops down on one knee before the Waitress.

Busboy: *(passionately)* "Shall I compare thee to a summer's day? Thou art more lovely and more temperate: Rough winds do shake the darling buds of May and summer's lease hath all too short a date."

Waitress: Joey! Did you get that from Dr. Elliot?

Busboy: Well he helped.

Gordon: A little.

Waitress: Did you mean what you said?

Busboy: Of course I did.

The two hold hands and look into each other's eyes.

Tall Man: If you two lovebirds are done, I need a refill!

The Waitress fetches the Tall Man's glass and refills it. Then she joins the Busboy at a corner booth. They talk quietly.

Gordon: *(To the Tall Man)* Are you happy?

Tall Man: No. Why should I be? I hate my job and… Why am I telling you?

Gordon: Maybe you have no one.

Tall Man: What do you mean, "No one?"

Gordon: To listen.

Tall Man: *(pause)* I don't have to talk to you or anyone!

The Obese Man gets up and staggers to the bathroom.

Gordon: I see.

Cook: "Hello, I love you! Won't you tell me your name?"

Tall Man: Will you shut up!

Cook: I'd rather sing.

Tall Man: Hey! Do you like your job?

Cook: Who? Me?

Tall Man: Yes! You!

Cook: No. I hate it. Why?

Tall Man: Well how do you stay in such high spirits during the day?

Just then, there is a loud crash from the bathroom. The waitress screams in surprise. Everyone turns except the Cook. The Busboy runs into the bathroom.

Cook: Well, let me tell you. When you've slammed your fingers in a waffle iron as many times as I have; you begin to not care anymore.

The Busboy rushes out. He returns with pallid expression.

Busboy: There's a dead man in the bathroom…

The waitress begins to cry. The Busboy consoles her. The Tall Man calls 911. Gordon begins to pray silently. The Cook seems callused to the situation.

Tall Man: Hello? 911? Yes, I wish to report an incident… *(Trails off)*

Cook: "Hello, I love you! Won't you tell me your name?" *Continues to cook.*

Curtain.

The Sinkhole
Ty Cronkhite

THE HOUSE WE MOVED into has a sinkhole in the driveway. I'm the only person in the house who has a car, and several days ago, I parked it in the sinkhole. As the snow melted with unseasonably warm weather, my car got sucked up. It was up to its axles in mud.

We talked many times about what might be under the sinkhole. It seemed to be covered with thick plywood under about a foot and a half of dirt, or in this case mud.

Some of us felt the house was haunted because of a terrible feeling of horror that overcame us whenever we went into the north room. Staying in that room was unbearable.

TY CRONKHITE lives somewhere in Albuquerque. He teaches and studies English Literature at the University of New Mexico.

We tried it one night, Ms. Cleda, Mr. Dobbs, and myself and found we could not do it even together. It was supposed to be Ms. Cleda's room, but she ended up storing a few of her things in it and staying in my room most of the time.

But the main thing is that the house seemed to have a dark history and mysterious footsteps in the night when someone would be in there alone. All of us heard them at one time or another. Mr. Dobbs said he was falling asleep on the couch one night when he heard some shuffling noises in the north room. He got up, shut the door and lay on the couch again. Five minutes later, he heard the footsteps. Clomp, CLUMP, clomp, CLUMP. It was as if the footsteps were coming right toward him. He kept his eyes shut as long as he could, and when he opened them the footsteps stopped. But the door to the north room was open about six inches.

And there were voodoo materials found in the attic. I have to mention that as well. One of the materials was a wax doll with a severed leg. In the same general area, tucked away in a corner was one well-worn work boot, size twelve. These things led us to believe that something awful had happened in this house.

By the time we had lived there about a year, we were convinced that a woman and two children lived there sometime in the recent past. The father and husband was an old man with a pockmarked face and a scraggly beard that covered a red, thick scar across his neck. The wound he received at the hands of a burglar who broke into the house and almost killed him. After that the old bastard - went by the name of Lanny Plooster - became mean as hell and padlocked his family inside the house every day when he went to work at the local meat packing plant.

That's where the voodoo materials came in. It was their only way out of the house that had become their prison. They warned him, but he never listened. He kept them locked up in there and beat them down almost every day. One day, while he was at work, they concocted this voodoo shit and he came home without his leg. An industrial accident.

Working at the meat packing plant, he didn't have a lot of money, so he constructed a prosthetic leg out of a fencepost, and lashed it to his oozing stump with leather belts and duct tape. Still, he just got meaner until one tragic night when he came at his wife with a meat tenderizer in his hand, drunk on cheap whiskey. She kicked his wooden leg out from under him, pulled it off, and beat him to death with it.

No one could have blamed her. It was a matter of self-defense.

Three days later the house was empty, and his body was never found. The woman and her two children moved away to Hollywood, where she became a famous actress and the children both criminal defense lawyers.

We all felt the story was based on facts we uncovered in research, but no one can remember who did the research or where the facts actually came from. Perhaps there was no basis for the story whatsoever.

But there is a fencepost missing in the front.

Although it was in the back of my mind earlier what might be buried under the sinkhole, my main concern was to get my car out of it so I could take back the movies and VCR we rented several weeks ago under the condition we return it the next day. I was trying to be proactive because the contract was in my name and I wanted to avoid contact with the law.

Getting my car out was not easy, and although my roommates offered to help, they weren't that serious and I thought of it as a challenge to get it out myself using only a shovel and some cardboard. I dug out around the tires and shoved the cardboard, some cat litter and tree branches under them for traction. I got in the car and tried various techniques to free it, the end result being that the cardboard, cat litter, and tree branches disappeared into the mud bog and the car became more stuck. I left it in reverse, and when I got out the wheels kept spinning in the muck, car going nowhere.

That gave me an idea.

I had an electric chain saw.

I cut more tree branches off the elm tree in our front yard, dragged them to the back and placed them under the rear wheels. I salvaged a piece of plywood to create a ramp from the floor of the sinkhole to solid ground. I drilled two holes in the floorboard of the car and attached a u-bolt just under the accelerator.

Just then, it turned midnight.

I tied a length of rope to the accelerator, ran it through the u-bolt on the floorboard, around the back of the seat and out the driver's side window. In this manner, I could put the car in reverse and manipulate the throttle with the rope while I pushed from the outside.

I put my back to the front of the car, leveraged my feet against something hard and pushed with all my strength. I held the rope in my teeth, so I could rev the motor by turning my head to the right. The rear wheels spun wildly and I could smell burning rubber. It was thirty-five degrees, and steam rose from underneath the car where the engine heated the muddy water in the bog.

"Shut the fuck up!" our neighbor yelled out his bedroom window.

Then I saw a well-worn work boot lashed to the end of the rotting fencepost I was using to brace my feet. I felt sick to my stomach as the story raged in my head. I jerked involuntarily to the right, pulling the accelerator to the floor just as the tires got traction and the car pulled itself up the ramp and out of the sinkhole. The rope was yanked out of my mouth. The Chevette backed down the driveway and into the street at a high rate of speed. With nothing there to support me, I fell backward in the mud.

There were no stars in the sky. The low clouds were illuminated by the city lights nearby.

"Shaddock."

"Huh, wha the he..."

"Mr. Shaddock, I'm not going to ask what you are doing."

I tilted my head to see a uniformed figure holding a clipboard. I didn't recognize him at first because the light was behind him and the frosty nighttime air was thick with haze. It was a surreal image at best.

But his voice betrayed his identity. It was Beckman. Officer Beckman of the Loveland Police Department. I knew him well, mainly from my work at Denny's, but also from the numerous citations he had offered me over the years.

He was good guy, for a cop.

"I've got a list of people. I'm supposed to arrest them for theft. Your name is on it," he told me.

He offered his hand to help me out of the pit. Out of the corner of my eye, I saw my car careening slowly down the dirt road toward an open field.

"You have some movies you rented from Blockbuster?"

"Yeah, I was just..."

"It's the VCR they're worried about, do you have it here?"

"Yeah, my car was stuck and I, well..."

I waved halfheartedly toward where my car had gone.

"I thought I'd save you some trouble. If you've got it I'll take it back for you and we won't mention this again. K? I'll cross you off the list."

"Sure, Beckman, thanks. Coffee's on me next time, right? Let me go get the stuff."

I went in the back door to get the movies and the video cassette player. Ms. Cleda met me at the door.

"The neighbors called the cops," she said and I disagreed. I tried to tell her the cop was just here for the movies.

"No, in front. It's about the noise. They think you are trying to bury something in the back yard."

Mr. Dobbs walked in from the front room. "Like a body," he said.

"Dammit, it's about the body, not the leg, the movies...he's in front now eh?"

"Yes, at the front door. I told them you were the owner."

I gathered the VCR and the tapes and took them to the front door where two sheriff deputies were waiting. Neither one of them was Beckman.

"You the owner?" one of them said when I opened the door wide to hand him the VCR and the movies.

"Not exactly, so, no. Uh, it's, they are someone else's. Rentals. I was just taking them back but my car was stuck on a leg and now I don't know where it is..."

He had his hands on the VCR, but I had not yet let go. He saw that I was covered in mud.

"Is this what you were trying to bury in the back yard?"

"No. It's mine. Give it back!"

He didn't want to give it back. Since he was stronger than I was, I let him have it.

A routine check on the serial numbers of the VCR revealed it had been reported stolen. Having been the one to sign the rental agreement, I was the main suspect. As my conversation with Deputy Dunderfeld continued, I began to feel progressively more arrested.

"We had reports of a chain saw, and that you were digging in the back yard."

"It was an electric chain saw. And the only thing that's buried in the backyard is a wooden leg."

I went on to explain how I was trying to dig my car out when I found Lanny's wooden leg and then how my car rolled out of the driveway out of control. I was just starting to make sense when we heard something outside.

"Oh crap," I said when I saw the backup lights on my car coming over an embankment from an empty field in front of the house. It veered to the right, to the left, crossed the road and crashed into the side of the sheriff's car.

"That the car you were talking about?" the deputy asked.

"Yes sir. That's my car."

I sat alone in the back of the patrol car for thirty minutes. He had the heater turned up full blast and I was sweating, my arms cramped behind my back. Over time, as I watched, Lanny's leg, which had been propped up in the mud, fell slowly back into the bog. The lights went off inside my house and a flickering blue light took over as Mr. Dobbs adjusted the antenna.

Arpeggio & Cinquain
Morgan Grayce Willow

Lover's Cinquain

I wake,
one arm stretching
over empty bed, one
spine curling around one dreamt form.
Missing.

The House Tea Pot

With pride
and oak leaves it
carves out its portion of
morning. Squat. Free of chips. Made in
China.

Twenty-Two

rainbow
degrees; Tarot
majors; syllables in
cinquain; city blocks between you
and me.

Predator

Rabbit.
Nothing left but
fur—tidy array banked
around absent body. Above:
eagles.

MORGAN GRAYCE WILLOW is the author of many books, including *Arpeggio of Appetite* (Finishing Line Press 2005), a volume of Cinquain. The 5-line, 22-syllable form was devised by an American poet, Adelaide Crapsey, (1878-1914). Morgan lives and teaches in Minneapolis.

The Glass Eater
Dan Coffey

I **EAT GLASS FOR A LIVING**. For the last couple of years, this has involved eating an ashtray an evening at a bar. I get the other men along the bar to wager that I can't eat an entire ashtray in one sitting. It takes me a couple of hours to do so, but I smash it into small shards and then slowly swallow them all. For this, I make anywhere from sixty to one hundred fifty dollars a night, tax-free. It's a tough job, but somebody's got to do it. At least I've got to do something, and this is the best way to make money I've found recently.

DAN COFFEY is a playwright, director and actor known for his work with *Duck's Breath Mystery Theater* and memorable characters like Dr. Science. Dan lives in Thailand.

I once met a man who ate an entire automobile. It took him almost two years to do so. He died shortly after he swallowed the last bolt, but the autopsy revealed eating the car was not his undoing. It was liver cancer, an infirmity that had been progressing for some time.

My line of work proves one thing: that you can accomplish seemingly impossible tasks if you break them down into small enough pieces and don't give up.

My wife is the unusual one in our family. She has a tattoo that stretches from her left shoulder to her right calf. I don't care much for tattoos, but I have to admit this one is well done, with all the colors and lines clear and defined. There is, however the troubling issue of the name of her beloved at the time of the procedure. The first man was named Hugh, which was skillfully redrawn to read Bart, then Burt, then Bert. For a while she had a thing for men whose first names began with the letter "B." The moniker remains Bert to this day, as the skin in that area was beginning to thin which permitted no more adjustment. Now, just above her buttocks surrounded by palm leaves, it reads "Bert," though she is now my wife and my name is Donald.

We have learned to accept each other with all our foibles. She is married to a man who eats ground glass for a living. I admit to myself that in her massage practice she sometimes strays over the line of what might be thought of as common decency.

The State of Emergency has been renewed again. I can't remember how many times they've said they're about to take away the curfew and stop interring the undesirables, but then they go and renew it for another ninety days. The Swat Teams are still coming and going, especially downtown, running in and out of local businesses and dragging more undesirables away to the huge, black trucks, the ones they park out back with the engines running.

Things could be worse. They say that almost everyone in Western Africa has already died of Ebola. The government channel keeps repeating that only because of rapid action by our peacekeeping forces were we spared the ionizing radiation that took out so much of Korea and Pakistan. So we're luckier than some, I guess.

I'd like to think that my line of work has protected me from disease. Quite a few of my friends have died in the past few years, but I seem to enjoy better health as time passes. Maybe there's something in the glass they use to make ashtrays that is beneficial, some sort of micronutrient. The guy who ate the car didn't get cured of his cancer, but maybe if he'd have stuck with ashtrays he would have been. Just a thought. Sometimes it pays to stick with something, no matter how sick of it you've become.

A few years ago, I went to the emergency room because I had a terrific headache. They ran about fifteen thousand dollars' worth of tests and finally told me I had a brain tumor. I laughed and walked out the door. Good luck getting me to pay. If they're right, I'd be insane to give them my money now when the debt will dissolve the moment I die. If they're wrong, then why should I pay them for a faulty diagnosis? The headache went away as soon as I had a couple of cups of coffee. Quitting caffeine is really difficult. That's why I have no intention of trying it again.

The more coffee I drink, the more quick-witted and talkative I become. There's a point where I can't think or talk any faster, and then it quickly nosedives into agonizing anxiety. You'd think I'd quit, or at least moderate, but such notions are foreign to my very nature. If it's worth doing, it's worth doing all the way, until you just can't do it anymore.

My wife and I only have sex once a year, on her birthday. To get herself in the mood she starts drinking at breakfast. By noon, she is no longer herself, adopting the character of Bette Davis, the thirties/forties film star. Even though English is not her first language, she does a very convincing impersonation, excelling especially in surveying the room and then proclaiming "what a dump!" Unfortunately, by evening, she has taken the role too far, and all the fun is gone, but that, unfortunately, is when she decides to get physical.

Our little game evolved from repeated viewings of our favorite Davis film, The Bride Came C.O.D. In one scene, Jimmy Cagney, an aviator who has discovered that Davis is a rich heiress, conspires to trap her in a cave until he can claim the ransom from her rich father. By kissing him, she tastes that he has been out of the cave and eaten something, so she realizes she has been deceived, and begins hitting him furiously. That's my wife's favorite part of the movie, and it was ours, until she took it as license and inspiration to attack me like a polecat, all in the name of fun.

At this point in the birthday revelry, she has dropped the Bette Davis accent and is simply grunting and howling in her native Russian. It was fun the first year. By now, like those Twilight vampire films, it has grown tired through repeated sequels. This last time, she stayed drunk for three days, coming to when she stopped mid-sentence while telling a story at a dinner we were having with friends. She had been talking in a pirate voice, a cartoonish characterization full of swearing and fake Cockney nautical phrases, when all of a sudden she asked in all seriousness "Where are we? What time is it? What are you doing here?" Needless to say, she put a damper on the evening and our guests soon found an excuse to check on the baby sitter.

But we're happy most of the time. I never told her about my diagnosis of a brain tumor, but I'm saving that in case I need a "get out of jail" card to get me out of a jam. Not all my behavior is blameless.

For most of my work-life, I worked in the furnace repair business. During that time, I never repaired a furnace, but rather gave the illusion of having done so, taking advantage of the fact that the obituary columns of local newspapers gave me plenty of leads to visit new widows about to endure their first winter alone. I would arrive at the house saying I was the man who had installed the furnace and was here to check the inverter before winter set in.

Usually I would bring along a good-looking young man as my assistant. He would ask the widow about her late husband, their children, and generally charm her and soothe her fears. She would always confide that she knew nothing about the furnace for that had been part of her late husband's domain.

I would bang around on the pipes in the basement for a few minutes, then come upstairs holding a filthy piece of equipment that I had surreptitiously brought with me in the first place, and proclaim that this was her lucky day because if she had fired that baby up it would have been sure to blow the house sky-high. These things usually run 700-800 bucks, but I had one in the truck that I would let her have for 350 cash, installation at no charge.

Nine out of ten times it worked and in the spring I could reprise the act again only with a roof repair version. Again, my assistant would praise the beauty of her grandchildren while I stomped around on the roof. This time I replaced the gutter diverticulator, which had rotted clear through. Usually I could only get two hundred for one of those imaginary babies, because the onset of winter is a lot scarier for most widows than that of summer.

When I tired of this, and the complaints reached the local police, I would move to another community with a large percentage of recent widows in their own homes, and harsh winters. The northern Midwest was my field of dreams.

But then I heard of a friend who was making great bucks running a modeling agency for teen-age girls in the Southwest. In this case, of course, their mothers were the marks, and all I had to do was supervise a pretty college-aged girl to work with the potential models. I dropped a lot of names and made many a vague allusion to showcases in Rio and Paris, but was careful to never make promises I could be held to.

One of my greatest breakthroughs was a series of affirmations sent to the fifteen-year old girls on their cell phones.

"If he thinks I'm pretty, then I am," was one of them. "My hair smells terrific and I feel just as good," was another. We had a good time making those up over shots and chasers in the motel room one night. Every teenage girl's life centers around her cell phone, so when it talks to her, she listens.

The mothers paid a monthly fee for the instruction, another for photographs and video demos, and we were able to get a dollar a day per client for the affirmations. It beat banging furnace pipes in the basement.

Eventually I know that I'll have to settle on a line of work that pays into social security. Once, when I was in my twenties, I was traveling in Mexico and I came upon an old American man who was staying in the same cheap hotel as me. He had been running a fever for days, trapped in his room, covered in blankets. I asked him if he'd seen a doctor. No, he had no money for that. Didn't he have social security? No, he'd been self-employed all his life. At the time I remember thinking "note to self: don't end up like him."

Now that the Department of Homeland Security has taken over all the local police departments, the War on the Homeless has taken on new vigor. I have no desire to spend my golden years interned in a camp in Utah or Nevada. I've heard rumors that there is a plan to send the Homeless and Undesirables to Paraguay, a country that has agreed to accept them for a fee, and then allow them to live in the Chaco, a region as difficult as any on the planet. Coincidentally, it is also where George W. Bush bought a hundred thousand acres of land just before he left office, in case he had to flee to a place with no extradition policy. Paraguay also welcomed many an ex-Nazi after World War II ended.

Well, I always wanted an excuse to work on my Spanish. Maybe there would be an upside to being shipped off to Nowhere Latin America. Room and board would be paid for by FEMA or some other Federal Agency.

There's already a stretch of Federal land in the Colorado Desert, east of the Salton Sea, where a de-commissioned army base, Slab City is home to a great number of nearly homeless year-around, though the population swells during the winter and gets very small during the summer, when the average temperature is 110 degrees. These people live in their vehicles or in tents. There is no water, electricity or sewer service, but the residents of Slab City make do.

There is another settlement nearby called East Jesus.

Most migration is caused by economic incentives. Many of us are economic refugees, though we're often reluctant to admit it. The reason I don't live in downtown Manhattan isn't because I don't enjoy museums and restaurants, it's because I can't afford the rents. The reason I no longer live in the States is because it's too damn expensive for what you get.

After some Internet research, I found several affordable and interesting places I could live in South America and Southeast Asia. Looking at making a major move in order to free myself from the grind of trying to make ends meet gave me a sudden rush of hope. Unfortunately, my wife wasn't as hopeful. "What a dump!" she intoned, wearily, as she wandered around the kitchen, looking for something to eat.

We decided to try Nicaragua first, then if that didn't seem like a possible home, Thailand. We bought tickets that very evening, but our mood was less than celebratory. I wasn't sure about Natasha's desire or motivation in this quest for change. In fact, I wasn't sure she even wanted to be with me anymore.

The morning we left, Natasha and I were hopeful for a few hours until we were stopped at the airport. As we went through immigration, we were separated. They took each of us to small offices on either side of a hallway. I was detained only briefly, but she was in there for almost half an hour. When she emerged, she wouldn't look at me, but she did manage to say "I'm not going," as she headed back to baggage claim. I chased her for a while, asking what happened and why had she changed her mind, but she was in no mood to respond. The last thing she said to me was "Have a nice life."

It turns out I never made it to Nicaragua, or Thailand for that matter. They took me off the plane in Miami and gave me two men as escorts who sat with me in some sort of lounge that felt a lot like a jail. We watched TV together. Fox and Friends, as I recall. Then I saw my picture fill the screen with the caption "ISIS terrorist captured at Miami airport" and my wife being interviewed by Sean Hannity and a blonde bimbo who pretended to be a tough-talking journalist unafraid to ask the important questions like what were my favorite TV shows and did I ever play video games and if so which ones?

My wife looked great under the TV lights, and then it occurred to me that this segment must have been recorded earlier, because she had had her hair styled in that way a couple of days ago. I asked my companion to the right if what we were watching was live TV, but he simply stared straight ahead, the only visible sign of life being the muscles in his jaw flexing as he slowly chewed gum. I suppose he had been instructed not to talk to me.

His companion also stared straight ahead, but at least he was watching TV, witnessing my wife telling the world that I was a high-ranking officer in ISIS, the spin-off terrorist group that split from Al-Qaida. He seemed interested in her story and impressed by the variety of realistic details with which she embellished her story.

I wanted to see and hear more, but then they cut to a diaper commercial. While young moms were beaming at their babies, I was escorted through a little-used door and out on the tarmac, where a military-type vehicle was waiting for me. We drove for a long time, nobody saying anything. Finally, we stopped in front of a Walgreens and a man joined us. He started speaking to me in another language, as if he expected me to speak it too.

"Is that Arabic? Are you speaking to me in Arabic?" I asked.

The man stopped talking. There was a long pause.

"If it is Arabic, then I don't know what you just said. If it isn't, I don't speak that language either."

He stared at me some more. Then he said in English, "We've got as much time as you do."

I shrugged. He shrugged back. We drove on in silence.

When we came to a clearing in a dense woods, it was already dark, but I could tell that it was some sort of air strip. And sure enough, there was an airplane waiting for us, a military plane. The seats faced backwards. The three of us were the only passengers. By this time, I had decided not to speak unless spoken to, and since no one was telling me anything, I had no idea of our destination, but I know we had been aloft for many hours before landing at an airstrip in the middle of a forest. Had we simply flown in circles all that time? No, the vegetation was different, the sounds of birds unfamiliar. Now it was morning, maybe a few hours past dawn. From there we drove a while in another vehicle, this time a Mercedes-Benz limo. Finally, we arrived at what seemed to be a hotel, built in the style of an alpine chalet.

I had slept on the plane, but not well, and so I was a bit groggy by the time we entered the building. The first people I saw looked strangely familiar. Then I realized who they were. George W. Bush, Donald Rumsfeld and Dick Cheney were hanging out near the bar at one end of a large dining room. In the middle of the room,

near the head of a long dining room table, slumped in a wheelchair and not talking to anyone, was Richard Nixon. Though my brain clouded, I did some quick figuring and estimated that he must be over a hundred. He looked every day of it. But here he was alive! And for some reason, someone had gone to great lengths to bring me to him!

Hillary Clinton and Condoleezza Rice entered the room dressed in tennis outfits and holding rackets. They looked in my direction and nodded to my two escorts, who quickly left the room. Condy came up to me.

"How was your flight?" she asked.

"No peanuts, no drinks, but at least we didn't crash," I answered.

Hillary seemed to find my response hilarious, because she snorted, and soon the others followed. Within seconds, even Nixon smiled, though he might have simply been suffering from gas.

"I can eat an ashtray if anybody would like to wager," I said.

Nobody said anything for a while. Nixon began to drool from the corner of his jowls.

Condy came in closer. "You want to eat an ashtray?"

"A glass one. It's what I do. You bet that I can't, and I do it anyway."

"How big an ashtray?" Rumsfeld asked.

"Anything you got."

There was some discussion among different groups in the room. Finally, Cheney snapped his fingers and a waiter came to me, carrying a large, glass ashtray.

"I'll need a hammer and a sock," I added. Someone translated for him in Spanish. He returned with those after a few minutes.

"By the way, where are we?" I asked Hillary.

"Paraguay," she responded.

It was all making sense now. I remembered the Bush family had purchased a large estate in Paraguay just before he left office.

As I began the process of reducing the ashtray to shards, another man in a wheelchair entered the room. It was Henry Kissinger, and he pulled up parking himself next to Nixon.

"I'll wager ten thousand dollars that he can,"

Rumsfeld announced. Cheney piped in "Five thousand that he can't." "I'll match that," Hillary piped in. Nixon started mumbling and then said very clearly "I'll suck Kissinger's cock if he can." The room erupted in laughter.

Then some men in colorful shirts carrying harps and oversized guitars entered the room and began singing what I assume was Paraguayan music. We were in for the long haul.

It took me six hours to eat such a large ashtray, and by the time I finished many of my hosts had drifted away, but Hillary and Condy stayed with me to the end. When I had a moment alone with Hillary, I whispered, "I thought you were on the other side."

"I stick with the winners," she whispered back.

Suddenly the party was over, at least for me. A couple of men in dark suits approached, one holding a black hood, which he put over my head. From there I was escorted out of the dining room and into another room, which might have been as big as the first, but since there was little sound, I couldn't tell. From there I was made to crouch and enter a smaller room, except it felt a lot like the same room. Then they took off the hood and I could see that I was inside a cage in the middle of another ballroom or dining room, only this one was dimly lit. This was to be my home for the next five days.

My first visitors were a Boy Scout troop. They were respectful and silent as they gathered around, whispering among each other until their leader told them I was a recently apprehended terrorist and that there had been a ten million-dollar bounty on my head. Then the whispering stopped and they simply stared. I smiled. Then I growled and they quickly backed off.

A Girl Scout troop came next, but they kept much more distance than the boys, and many of them refused to look at me at all, feigning interest instead in the windows and furniture of the room itself. After they left, I was served lunch, which I wolfed down. Then Condy came to see me.

"We want to thank you for your cooperation. Our campaign needed a victory and even though we know this is all entirely made up, well, so was our invasion of Iraq. A fully-functioning democracy is a difficult myth to maintain, and having you here is helping keep it afloat," she said.

"I don't remember agreeing to anything," I said.

"It was tacit. There will be a simulated execution in a few days and then you'll be handsomely rewarded and relocated. What's your feeling about Indiana?"

"Don't know much about it. I was born there, but we moved to Chicago when I was still a toddler."

"We know that. Peru, Indiana is interested in helping us with this. Real estate is a real bargain in Peru. Not a bad place, either. It's everything wrong and right about small town America."

"Isn't it easier to hide in a big city?"

"That's what they say, but if you move to a place like Peru, Indiana, everybody's glad to see you. As long as you make a good first impression, you're golden. If you tell them you're a nudist or an atheist or you believe homosexuals should marry, then we'll just have to relocate you again."

"Lightning bugs on a summer night. Listening to the ball game on the radio."

"Beats Gitmo any day."

"But why me in the first place?"

"You made the mistake of pissing off your wife. She's a well-connected woman with some strong opinions of her own, especially about you. When she made up her mind, she made up her mind. Fortunately, her offer to us came at a time when we could use an unconventional person such as yourself. One with no support network to speak of. Few close friends. A guy like you can disappear and cause nary a ripple."

I saw her point. Instead of gaining a sort of freedom from not cultivating ties, I had become an invisible, forgotten man. Not the kind of guy you need to torture or repress, because I wasn't trying to do much of anything at all. I was a thorn in no one's side; instead, I was a shadow creeping along the wall. My lack of zest had put me in the position to be the perfect puppet.

Well this puppet was going to find some way to break his strings, or at least tangle them. I had to lay low and wait for opportunity. Despite her assurances otherwise, would I be executed in a few days? Probably not, but who knows what other lies Condy could tell with a straight face?

I thought I would lose my mind when they started showing my favorite kids show from the fifties, Andy's Gang on the big screen TV that filled most of the opposite wall. Sixty years later, I still found the character of Froggy to be terrifying. And Andy Devine was hideous. I kept waiting for him to clear his throat, but he only grew hoarser over time. The show was so mind-numbingly stupid that even at the age of five I must have known something was deeply wrong here. When they had nothing to show they cut back to a stock shot of the kids in the audience laughing dementedly. Froggy would use his magic powers for evil to confuse Andy (no difficult task) and make him do what he never intended.

Yes, Cheney and Rumsfeld had done their research well. How many of our tax dollars had gone into determining which television shows their future torture victims had watched as children?

The television torture went on for eight hours or so. Every once in a while a nurse with a clipboard would quietly enter the room and record my reactions. At first, I waved at her and smiled, but later on, I ignored her. The last few times I must have been asleep, though my sleep was fitful, as every time Froggy laughed his horrible laugh I convulsed.

The next morning a beautiful young woman was staring at me. She was dressed in a brightly colored polyester uniform, the kind favored by fast food employees.

"A broken old man with shattered dreams," she cooed. "We get a lot of those. Do you want breakfast?"

"Pancakes," I replied. "I was dreaming about pancakes."

"This is your lucky day!" she assured me. "Smothered in imitation maple syrup, with a side of greasy sausage links, just the way you like 'em."

Unfortunately, she brought me no pancakes, but instead continued to tease and make fun of me the rest of the morning. Then a man brought me a Burger King Double Whopper Combo Meal with bacon, large fries and a Chocolate Shake. It amazed me that such a thing could be found in Paraguay, but I inhaled it and felt just as bad as I usually do afterwards. It was sort of comforting in a nostalgic way.

Amaya Mokini
Stephen L. Snook

STEVE SNOOK is the author of *One Degree South* (Rocket Science Press 2014), source of this fictional vignette. Formerly from St. Paul, Steve served as a Peace Corps volunteer in Gabon. He has a PhD in political science and lives in Burlington, Vermont.

EARLY THE NEXT MORNING, Hector roared up Charlie's driveway driving Twisted Sister, a light wooden frame covered with plastic mesh assembled in the pickup bed. Justine would ride in comfort on a foam rubber mattress. The mesh would allow the air to flow, keeping her cool and diffusing direct sunlight so she wouldn't burn.

Charlie carried Justine to the truck. For days, she had been too weak to walk, too light, too frail. Cradled in his arms on this morning, however, she was alert. "I'm sorry," she said, her voice as dry as dust. "I knew growing old would be bad. I just didn't know it would happen this soon."

Charlie did his best to laugh for his beautiful fighter. Her mother had braided her hair, and Charlie was touched by the hopeful act. He set Justine gently on the tailgate, climbed up, lifted her again and carried her on his knees onto the makeshift bed. Justine's mother, Mama Angélique, still in mourning, still wearing widow's weeds, crawled in alongside, put a pillow beneath her daughter's head and covered her with a bright blue print pagne.

Jonas reached under the mesh past Charlie and squeezed Justine's hand. "You'll be all right," he said to his sister. "You'll be all right."

The twin brothers climbed in last, and Dabrian shut the tailgate. "Everything will be all right," he said to the boys. "We're going to save Justine, bien sûr."

Timo and Hector waved grimly as Dabrian drove Twisted Sister away. Jonas rode in the cab, to give directions.

As they pulled out of the Cité de la Caisse, Justine asked Charlie to feel her swollen abdomen. When he put his hand on the ghastly bulge, it yielded like a water balloon. It horrified him to feel.

"Does it hurt when I press on it?" he asked.

"No. The pain moves around, like an animal inside me. Sometimes it's in my lower back. Other times it's in front, down low or higher up toward my chest. Some days it's a pain so sharp that it makes me curl up in a ball. Other days, it throbs and makes me sick to my stomach."

The prescription painkillers helped, but Justine didn't like how they put her to sleep. She only took them when she couldn't stand the pain. When they crossed the river, leaving the city of Franceville behind, she took a tablet, because the truck's vibrations were making the pain worse, and soon she was blessedly asleep. Dabrian drove slowly, not wanting to jostle Justine, and because the mesh could not withstand the beating of the wind at high speed. He passed through his village, Ondili. When he came to the Talking Tree, the massive iroko tree whose spirit protected surrounding villages from French road builders, Dabrian continued east through the junction onto the paved highway leading north.

Justine slept all the way to Lékoni, two hours, and was still asleep as they continued north, the road ahead wet with rain ahead of them. Charlie had brought a tarp in case of rain, but on that day, rainy season showers fell everywhere save on them. Dabrian set out across the rolling sand hills beyond Lékoni, the grass sparkling green, the early afternoon sky bright blue. Twisted Sister made slow progress north on the rough track. Eventually, Justine awoke and asked for water, talking drowsily with Charlie in French, then for a while with her mother in Téké before falling asleep again.

Twisted Sister crawled past a succession of Peace Corps villages, each with evidence of work on a new school underway. Volunteers and their workers waved and wondered about the strange-looking frame in the back of the Peace Corps truck that usually stopped, but this time didn't.

At Jonas's direction, Dabrian turned east on a faint track toward the Congo. In the bed of the truck beside Justine, facing backward, Charlie noted the turn. Blaise and Gérard wore an identical look of juvenile ferocity. Mama Angélique kept close watch over her daughter. Jonas, riding in the cab, guided Dabrian to their destination. Charlie wouldn't have known what to do without the others here with him. He would have been losing his mind.

Twisted Sister had climbed a high ridge onto the watershed separating Gabon from Congo. In the near distance in the haze was a low conical mountain.

"There is Amaya Mokini," said Jonas. "Look down there by the stream at the foot of the mountain. The village where we are going is our sacred ancestral site."

Dabrian descended into the valley. "All the huts are built with thatch," he said. They reminded him of schoolbook illustrations of Iroquois longhouses. "There are no metal roofs."

"Yes, they are built in the traditional way," said Jonas. "This is a pure place. All who live in this village are untainted. There are no metal roofs, no plywood doors, not one nail in any of the houses. Nothing in this place has come from the white man."

Entering the isolated community, a dozen houses woven from fronds of raffia palms, Dabrian thought to himself, This is where I'm supposed to be, here in this village, at this time. Before he could bring Twisted Sister to a full halt, a group of scrawny, knobby-kneed, barefoot children surrounded the truck, grinning and yammering at the curiosity of visitors. The children were visibly less well-nourished than the children in Ondili, Dabrian's village. A thin-limbed, pot-bellied boy toddled over, naked, holding an older girl's hand. A handful of men and women wrapped in pounded raffia cloth approached the truck. Dabrian got out, a black man with physical features no one recognized.

Charlie provoked gasps when he stood, a giant white man. Justine crawled to the tailgate on her hands and knees, and he lifted her tenderly, his face brave for her, masking the anguish he felt. She wanted to walk, and he supported her, going slowly behind the others to a hut set apart a little distance off.

A small, old woman sat on a stool outside her house in a dull-colored raffia cloth sheath, a second raffia cloth around her shoulders as a shawl, a woven raffia hat, and multiple necklaces adorned with red feathers, bird claws and white cowry shells.

Dabrian had last seen the old woman in the dream, waving him ashore. He had met her in Okouya, the ngaa-bwa who unleashed his atura afou, the old woman who ruled this last reserve.

She acknowledged Dabrian with a nod to say she had known they were coming. Dabrian saw it in her shrewd and wrinkled face.

She turned her gaze on Charlie, and studied him with hooded eyes. She began to speak.

Jonas translated. "She says she knows you, Charlie. She was in Okouya while you were sick. She says there is a hole in you. Terrible things done to you when you were a child burned a hole that you have tried to plug by caring for no one. Now you have learned to care for another, and the hole is closing. You are becoming fully human. She says you must breathe easy now, for you have come to a place where people are healed."

Charlie sobbed from the sudden rush of relief, glad that no one looked at him. The ngaa-bwa led the way into her hut. It had no windows and no interior rooms. It took a while for Charlie's eyes to adjust to the gloom. Justine lay down wearily on a mat beside a small fire. Soot caked the underside of the low curving thatch roof. Charlie knelt beside Justine and touched her hip, her shoulder, and winced to feel her bones. "I love you," he whispered. Justine opened her dark eyes and smiled.

Charlie and Dabrian sat side-by-side on a small, short bench, their knees under their chins. Jonas and the twins sat on stools. Mama Angélique sat on the mat beside Justine, stroking her daughter's forehead. Scorched stones ringed the fire. Against one wall, shelves fashioned from saplings held the healer's wares, antlered animal skulls, clumps of feathers and strange wooden things, leather sachets and rows of blackened clay pots.

The ngaa-bwa squatted and spoke to Mama Angélique. Jonas translated. "She has asked to hear Justine's problem."

Mama Angélique spoke at length, describing the painful swelling in her daughter's abdomen and the futile medical tests of the doctors. When she finished, the ngaa-bwa produced a shard of mica and gazed into it for some time, before placing her small strong hand on the thin pagne covering Justine's swollen belly. She closed her eyes. After a few moments, the old woman began to moan, stiffening as a shudder ran through her. Suddenly, she flung open the pagne. The swelling on Justine's abdomen moved like a creature alive. Horror-struck, Charlie turned to Dabrian in a speechless rage that pleaded for the ngaa-bwa to remove the hideous thing.

The old woman put her ear on the undulant swelling, listening for a time before mercifully closing the pagne. Then she rose to her feet, rooted through the shelves for two leather sachets and a soot-covered pot, which she filled with cloudy liquid from a gourd. She squatted on her heels by the fire, and balanced the pot on a rock while the liquid heated. With intense concentration, like a puzzler sorting complex pieces, she pointed at Justine's belly and spoke.

Dabrian understood. "There is a scorpion inside her."

Charlie reacted like he'd been slapped. "What?"

"There is a scorpion in her," said Jonas. "A scorpion in her womb."

Charlie was stunned. "How can that be?"

"It's the curse," answered Jonas. "The scorpion has been stinging her. The poison from many, many stings is causing the swelling and the pain."

Dabrian saw Charlie's muscles bulge with a need to lash out, to punish someone, and he remembered what had happened the moment his atura afou first stirred, and became manifest, when the old woman here placed his hands on the forehead of a woman in a shroud. Scorpions had come swarming out of the winding sheet. A scorpion, he thought. Of course.

"She wants us to know her name," said Jonas. "She is called Eloguemonono Alouo. She is skilled in the old ways, and she will help us. She says someone in Okouya did this, someone very evil. She asks us to remember that she was called to Okouya. No one asked her to come. She was called. She says she was unable to eradicate all the evil she found. There was too much, and it was very strong. The person who did this has very strong unkébé. She is going to give Justine some medicine now. When next Justine urinates, the poison will be expelled, and the swelling will go down."

"She'll be cured?" Charlie asked, wanting intensely for Justine's ordeal to end.

Jonas repeated Charlie's question. The old woman answered. Jonas translated. "She says Justine won't be cured until the scorpion is expelled from her womb. Someone who wants to kill her put it inside her. The scorpion has built a nest. It will not be easy to flush out. We must begin by learning the name of the sorcerer."

Dabrian looked at Charlie, horrified, enraged and helpless to do anything. He looked at Justine's mother, resolute, her thin face etched from a lifetime of hardship. At last someone had explained what was wrong with her daughter, and finally a plan could be made. Charlie's face clenched in fury. He wasn't sure he actually believed there was a scorpion inside Justine stinging her, but someone was making her suffer and he wanted to know who that was. He wanted violent revenge.

When the pot began to boil, the ngaa-bwa sprinkled in a pinch of dried leaves from one of the leather sachets and a pinch of red powder from the other. She peered into the steam rising from the pot, concentrating, saying nothing. After a few minutes, she took the pot off the flames, her short fingers insensitive to the heat, and set it in the sand. She breathed on it until the steam had dissipated, then gazed into the potion and described the layout of Okouya, drawing an L-shape in the sand. She put her finger over the spot in the village where the sorcerer lived.

Jonas translated. "She says a man who always wears a blue hat has been making unkébé in secret for many months. A big man, a politician, hired him to kill Justine."

"I want him killed!" Charlie bellowed, in a voice Dabrian had never heard him use. Both of them knew who it was, the man in the blue hat, the man-bat Dabrian had seen approaching Justine smiling, with mischief up his sleeves.

Eloguemonono Alouo resumed talking, and Dabrian closed his eyes, listening to the old woman's voice. An image materialized, waves of faint colors, and Dabrian saw the man-bat in Okouya wearing an incongruous blue yachting hat, and saw something fly into the man-bat's mouth.

He opened his eyes and saw the ngaa-bwa speaking directly to Charlie. Jonas translated. "The unkébé requires a soul to eat, Charlie. Your secret enemies chose Justine because she is your girlfriend, and she is a stranger to Okouya."

"But why kill her? Why not kill me?" Charlie's eyes narrowed, his jaw clenched, incredulous, confused and so enraged he wanted to tear the whole world apart.

"Killing Justine will accomplish two things.

First, it will enhance the politician's power, which is their main purpose. Second, it will exact revenge against you for something you did."

Charlie pounded his fists like sledgehammers on his knees. "How can this be my fault?"

Mama Angélique wailed at what the ngaa-bwa said next, and Jonas translated.

"The spirits of two grandmothers have been protecting Justine, but they are not strong enough to resist for much longer."

"What are we going to do?" Charlie cried. He wanted action. "Ask her, Jonas. Ask her!"

And Jonas rattled off the question.

Squeeze My Hand
Kitty Baker

SQUEEZE MY HAND

Don't tell!
my younger sister Sil insists.
Don't tell Mom.
No one in our family.
Nor anyone back home.
Never, ever.
Promise, please!
I can handle this.

I promise, drunk on her trust in me
to be sole keeper of her secret.

Occasions pass.
Easter.
Mother's Day.
An endless Memorial weekend.
July's celebration of independence.
The family reunion of the decade.
Each time Sil calls
home with her excuses.
The birthday they share,
her 19th, Mom's 44th,
celebrated blind and sober
over long-distance lines.

Sil and me
off-campus college coeds.
City sisters now.
I play the roll of coach.
Give up smoking, saving
toward bills she'll owe.
Sew smocks,
camo for the swell of her belly.

KITTY BAKER is a professional writer and local food advocate. She lives in rural southeast Minnesota outside of Lanesboro.

Hide her in my closet when
back-home guests drop by.
She nests into dirty laundry
until the coast is clear.

We take the birthing classes.
We practice fake contractions.
I squeeze her arm, imprinting bruises.
She concentrates on breathing
leaving the senses of her body
until at last,
she feels no pain.
We perfect Lamaze techniques
as summer wanes.

Labor Day.
A clockwork of cramps bring on
Sil's practiced trance.

Helpless, scattered,
I hold her hand and issue orders,
Squeeze when you can't stand it.
I time her quiet desperation,
minutes mounting into hours.
Each contraction
more raging than the last.
Her fingers curl, a death grip.
My palm, squeezed senseless
surrenders chips of ice as consolation.
I pray as we did in childhood
losing track
of what I should and shouldn't say to
her, to God or anyone.
Breathe! I cry
as the secret baby finally crowns
and births
and the three of us are bawling
and Catholic Charities arrives
to spirit a lovely infant girl away.

Years trickle by.
A string of Mother's Days.
A rash of newborn nieces, nephews
seeds another generation.
Sil concentrates on leaving the senses of her body
welcomes each newcomer to the family
as she never could the lovely
nameless missing one.

Her secret holds,

beguiling Mother, siblings
and everyone back home.
Warding off a burden of regrets
as cancer lays its claim on Mom
keeping her from ever turning 58
from ever knowing of
her first true grand brood.

Re-enter
the baby girl, now 27.
Tell me who I am!
This lovely one insists.
Sil goes closet mode –
a whiff of dirty laundry.
Stoic. She refuses.
Resists.

Tell me, damn it! The girl persists,
until,
at last
Sil's never-ever vow gives way.
Maternal gravity erupts.
For one lone moment
unrequited mother-daughterness
breaks all barriers of
sound and will.
Orgasmic.
The moment passes.
The newborn reunion –
its breath sucked from tender lungs –
asphyxiates.
Smothers.
Aborts.
Damned if I will ever understand.
The long-delayed birthright,
even now, can never be.

Another dozen Mother's Days
pass without due celebration.
Another cancer makes another claim.
Another mother rushes
toward an early grave,
my little sister Sil.
Insistent still, *I can handle this!*
She will not risk
judgments nor rejection
closets herself from all estrangements
that could complicate her passing.
And there's no time
to practice feel-no-pain routines.

I can barely hear her whisper
as she tucks her palm in mine
and coughs up my birth-coach line,
Squeeze when you can't stand it.

I sit with her, I clock
her breathing, each draw
less quenching than the last
Her lungs wheeze,
her chest rattles,
her fingers quiver, too weak to curl.

Helpless, scattered,
I scramble for more morphine.
Breathe! I order her
and hold my breath
and squeeze her hand.
A death grip
at last
shatters
the promise-you-won't-tell
of so long ago.

LEE HENSCHEL JR. is the author of a 1981 collection, *Short Stories of Vietnam*. The featured short fiction is an excerpt from his 2014 novel, *The Sailing Master, Book One: Coming of Age* (Rocket Science Press). Lee lives in Minneapolis.

Punishment
Lee Henschel Jr.

SEVERAL DAYS passed until Lieutenant Rainey appeared on the quay leading his lot of pressed men. Even before Mr. Starling stepped on the quay for inspection, he ordered the bosun's mate to strip the men and hose them down. Soon they all stood naked as jays and dripping wet, their backs turned to the catcalls and whistles coming from the randy women who'd come to observe.

Mr. Starling took pity on the pressed men and ordered the marines to chase off the crowd. Only then did he proceed with his examination.

Three men were young, not above twenty. One man was nearly too old to serve. And one fellow was a halfwit and discharged prompt. When Mr. Starling was satisfied, he ordered the men issued their slops. The black tunics and grey dungarees elevated their spirits and they went onboard willingly, to be met at the entry port by Coutts, who entered each man's name in the register. I heard Coutts pronounce them all landsmen and meant to deduct their first month's wages against their new togs. He then turned them over to Lance Corporal Marley, acting as *Eleanor*'s sergeant-at-arms. The corporal introduced each of them to his starter, and led them below.

I stood at the fife rail, watching Reggie follow the poor men below. I liked Reggie. He seemed capable of talking to me without yelling or telling me to shut my mouth. I felt safe to ask him questions. And I had many, so I followed him down through the officers' mess and into his cubby hole. As loblolly Reggie also served as ship's apothecary and he worked and slept where the physics and such were stored, just across from the first officer's cabin. When I knocked, he looked up from his tiny desk and smiled.

"Harriet! I wondered when you might come pay me a visit."

"Hello, Reggie. May I come in?"

"It's cramped, but if you step in and close the door we'll have a bit more room. I must finish this first. I'll only be a moment."

He began to write, his quill scratching distinctive as he drew it across the ledger. When he set the quill down I spoke.

"Reggie?"

"Yes, Harriet."

"When did you learn to write? And to read?"

"Oh, I was about your age. A bit younger, I suppose."

"Then it's not too late for me to learn how?"

"Of course not."

"Mum taught me numbers when I helped at her loom. And letters, too, but not so much. I should like very much to learn proper."

"Then I'm sure you shall."

"What are you writing now?"

"The names of the men who just came onboard. Mr. Starling requires me to keep our own ledger. To make sure."

"Sure of what?"

"Of Coutts. The man keeps two ledgers. One is for the ship. That ledger is an official register for pay tickets, clothing allotments, and all sundry items. The account is a necessary record, done up proper. Coutts also keeps a ledger for himself, though. All pursers do it. And when . . ."

We heard Marley yelling at the new men, bullying them into the officers' mess and lining them up. Reggie opened his door a crack and we peeked out. The deck was empty but for the press. A sorry lot. Another man joined them now, one I'd not seen before. Without delay a lieutenant stepped from the first officer's cabin. It wasn't Rainey. The fellow walked slow and with stormy intent, stopping before the men, measuring them in a pronounced silence, his face dour and dark. The lieutenant drew a deep breath and burst out in a long and strident shriek of insults, howling high and roaring most low, calling them the worst stinking collection of miscreants he'd ever smelled. He grew more livid by the second, spittle flying and the men cowering. His rant went on and on and the men quaked and cowered, the oldest one crying openly. The lieutenant paced forth and back, flailing his arms, shaking his fist and shaming them no end until, without warning, one of the men, the one I'd not seen before, charged him, screaming that he'd had enough and would take no more. He raised a fist as if to strike and that's when the lieutenant took one step back, drew his pistol, and shot the man in the heart. The man fell to his knees, then flat to the deck, his hands pressed over his heart, blood seeping between his fingers. The men stood dumb until one of them mumbled The Lord's Prayer, followed by an agony of silence.

Ding-ding. Ding.

One-thirty in the afternoon watch. I'd just seen a man shot dead. I began to weep. Reggie laid a trembling hand on my shoulder. The lieutenant lowered his pistol, walked slowly over to the man, and calmly gazed down at him.

"Dead, b'God." He turned to face the pressed men. "Let this be the first thing you learn about serving in the Royal Navy. If you raise a hand to strike an officer you will be shot dead." He put his pistol away. "Now then, any questions?"

No questions, of course, so he ordered Marley to march the men away. When they were gone the lieutenant went to the cabin and closed the door, leaving the body on the gun deck. Uncovered and unattended. All went quiet.

"May I get up now? The floor has slivers and I've got one stuck in me arse from me fall of death."

Rainey and the other officer came out then, laughing. They helped the dead man stand, and Rainey patted him on the back.

"And an epic death it was, Dewey."

"Thank you, sir."

Dewey took out a rag and wiped his hands of blood. Not blood though, only water dyed red.

"Most convincing, Dewey. I never once saw you breathe."

"Holding me breath's me specialty, sir."

Rainey turned to the other fellow. "And you, Hodge, can't you just play the nasty officer, though?"

"Thank you, sir. I played it just as you wrote it."

"You did indeed, and with great fire. I began to feel a bit sorry for the beggars."

"Yes, sir. I only wish we could have played to a bigger crowd."

"Not for this performance. I made sure the mess was cleared for a private audience. But you've earned your wages this day."

Rainey fished in his waistcoat and took out a crown, shiny new, and flipped it to Hodge.

"You will go ashore now. But next time I've a need to tyrannize the press you're the lads for me. You may be sure of it."

Say Cheese
Michael Edwin Q.

LISA WALKED OUT ON THE PORCH, placed the tray on the table, and started handing out glasses. "Here you are, Daddy, plenty of sugar and extra lemon the way you like it." She handed a glass to her husband. "Here you are, Bob, no sugar." She looked across the porch at her teenage son, staring out at the lake. "Would you like some, Kevin?"

"No."

"No what?"

"No, I don't want some."

"That's not what I meant, and you know it."

"Leave the boy alone," said Bob. "He's at that age."

Kevin rolled his eyes. "Why do I have to spend half my summer every year in this dump?"

"Because you're part of this family," said Bob.

"I didn't ask for that," complained Kevin.

"Well, you're stuck with it," his mom replied.

"I hate it here," continued Kevin. "There ain't nothing to do."

MICHAEL EDWIN Q. won the 2013 Art Affair Literary Award. He has been writing professionally since he was twelve and lives in Dallas, Texas.

His mother corrected his English. "There *isn't anything* to do."

"That's what I just said," pouted Kevin.

His grandfather, Bill, took exception to this, put down his glass and sat up in his chair. "What do mean, there isn't anything to do? There are plenty of things to do?"

"Yeah, and they're all stupid. Name one thing to do that ain't stupid," spouted Kevin.

"What are you saying," said Bill, in amazement and disbelief. "You're grandmother and I bought this lake house the first year we married. We'd spend every chance we could up here. Before your momma was born, we'd come up here with friends. We'd swim, and fish, and go canoeing, go for walks around the lake, hike up in the mountains, and have cookouts. There are lots of great things to do here. It's a good thing your grandmother isn't alive to hear you say such things."

"Gee, I'm sorry I said anything. Excuse me for living," said Kevin.

"Don't let him get you, Pop," said Bob. "He'll learn."

Just then, Kevin's two younger siblings, Chrissie – ten and William – eight, came running onto the porch and up to their grandfather.

Chrissie had something in her hands. "Grandpa, what kind of camera is this?" she asked.

He took it from her and laughed. "Why, this is my old camera. You don't see cameras like this too often. It needs film. Where did you find this?"

"We found it in the basement," replied Chrissie.

"Now, you two know you're not supposed to play in the basement," said Linda.

Little William spoke up in their defense in true lawyer fashion. "We weren't playing; we were exploring."

"I don't care what you two were doing; I don't want you down in that basement."

"How does it work?" asked Kevin.

Everyone turned and looked at Kevin, surprised he was interested in anything other than complaining.

Bill explained, "Well, you put the film in back here, then you look through the viewfinder, when you see something you want a picture of you press this button. The light goes through the lens and the image is captured on the film. You develop the film, then put the film in an *Enlarger*, shoot the image on some special paper. Then you soak the paper in a bath of special chemicals and you've got a picture."

"Can you show me how to use it?" asked Kevin.

"Yeah sure, just come with me to the basement and I'll teach you everything you need to know to be a *Shutterbug*."

"Shutter what?"

"I'll explain as we go," said Bill.

As the two went into the house, Linda and Bob stared at each other in amazement and then broke out laughing.

Down in the basement, Bill took Kevin to the far back where there was a table with a strange contraption on it.

"This is your *Enlarger*. You see the hooks in the ceiling. That's how I used to turn this area into a dark room. I'd hook up that curtain all around this table." He pointed at a pile of black fabric. "You got to do most of your developing in darkness."

"I want to take some pictures and develop them, show me how," said Kevin.

"Well, you got all the chemicals and materials here, but they're old. I got into photography just after I married your grandmother. The film, the paper, and the chemicals are all older than you, heck they're older than your mother. I doubt if they're any good."

"But we can try," said Kevin.

"Yeah, I guess we can at least try."

Bill slowly and carefully walked Kevin through the science of film developing.

"Lunch is ready," Linda called down the basement stairs.

"We'll be up in a minute," Bill hollered up to his daughter. But they were too inolved in what they were doing and never came up. Bill found some old negatives of his daughter when she was a little girl, and they made five by seven prints of them. At Linda's insistence, the two came up for dinner.

In the dining room, Kevin proudly showed off the pictures he and his grandfather developed. Both his parents praised his handiwork, not only because they were pleased to see their son interested in something other than loafing around, and willing to learn.

Linda eyed the photos. "I remember that summer. That was the summer that Millie and Dick Anderson and Helen and Ray Taylor came and stayed here with us for two full weeks. I was the only child, and the center of attention. I'll never forget that swimsuit; it was green with white and pink flowers."

Bob looked over his wife shoulder. "Real nice work, you guys."

"It was a group effort," said Bill. "I took those shots a million years ago, but Kevin did the developing. It's his turn tomorrow. The camera's loaded and ready to go. He doesn't need my help anymore. Whatever shots he takes, he can print them by himself. He is, from this day on, an official *Shutterbug*."

"The word *Shutterbug* comes from a part of the camera called the *Shutter*," Kevin announced proudly.

"Is that so?" said Linda, pretending not to know what the term meant, and inwardly pleased to see the change in her son.

"Mom?" asked Kevin. "When you get up tomorrow morning to make breakfast, could you wake me too? Grandpa says morning light is the best time to take pictures."

Bill leaned across the table towards Bob. "What I don't understand is how all that equipment, film, paper, and chemicals can still be good. It's amazing."

True to his word and the amazement of his parents, Kevin was up at dawn. He kissed his mother good morning, grabbed a slice of toast, and was out the door heading for the morning light with his camera dangling from his neck.

For the rest of the family it was a day like any other. After breakfast, Linda and Bob took Chrissie and little William for a short hike along the lake. Grandpa Bill sat on the porch drinking coffee and reading the morning newspaper. When it warmed, the children changed into their swimsuits. Linda and Bob sat in lounge chairs and watched the children swim. Near noon, Linda went back to the house and prepared a picnic basket, also leaving a sandwich on the table for her father.

The four of them walked along the east side of the lake to the big rock where they had their picnic. Linda went back to the house to have a lie-down in their room, while Bob took the children out in the rowboat. Grandpa Bill took a long nap in the hammock with his face covered with the morning paper.

Later, Linda got up and went to the kitchen to prepare dinner. As the sweet smell of a cake baking drifted from the house, like responding to a bugle call, Bob and the children returned; Grandpa Bill woke and sat on the porch reading a paperback.

All in all, it was a good day, with one unusual feature. Now and then, the sound of a camera shutter opening and closing split the air. A person would turn to see Kevin with his eye pressed to the viewfinder of the camera, taking snap shots of everyone and everything; he seemed to be everywhere. Once he'd snapped off two rolls of film, he went back to the house and down to the basement to process the film.

"Kevin, dinner time!" his mother shouted down the basement stairs.

"Not now, Mom; I'm right in the middle and I can't stop!"

"Kevin, you come up here this minute."

"But it will all be ruined!"

"Let the boy go, Linda," said Bob. "I've never seen him enthused about anything so much in his life."

Later, once it grew dark, the rest of the family went into the living room to relax. Grandpa Bill sat alone on the porch, watching the night sky. Kevin emerged from the basement. He walked onto the porch and handed his grandfather a stack of black and white, five by seven photos.

"I remember that summer," laughed Bill. "It was about two years before your mother was born. Look at this one of your Grandmother getting ready to take a swim. She was a peach. Oh, and this one. That's the Anderson's, Millie and John. I became friends with him in college. This one is of the Taylors, Helen and Ray. They were all fun people. That was a great summer. Gee, they're all dead now; I'm the only one left. These are great pictures, Kevin, where did you find them?"

"I didn't," he said solemnly. "Those are the pictures I took today. When I developed the film, that's what appeared on the paper."

Bill looked them over again and shook his head. "Kevin, think about what you're saying. It's impossible. You must have somehow got the negatives mixed up."

Kevin walked to the edge of the porch, looked up and pleaded to the stars. "Why do adults tell you to speak the truth; but when you do they don't believe you!"

"Alright, alright," said Bill. "I'll tell you what. Tomorrow, you and I are going out with the camera and shoot a roll of film, and then we'll develop them together, and then we'll know."

"And then you'll know, because I saw what I saw and I know what I know," said Kevin as he went back into the house, leaving Bill with the photos.

The next morning both grandfather and grandson grabbed a slice of toast and were out the door to catch the first sunrays of the morning. Bill let Kevin take all the pictures, having him try to take pictures similar to the ones he took the day before. By noon, all the shots on the roll of film were used. They went down to the basement. Only this time, Bill did all the darkroom work. When he was done, he held a stack of freshly developed black and white, five by sevens. Every picture was of the space Kevin took the picture of, but not the time. The people in the photos were Grandma Christine, the Andersons, and the Taylors, some fifty plus summers ago.

"Now do you believe me?" asked Kevin.

"This can't be happening," said Bill. It's impossible. Grab another roll of film; we're going out to take more pictures."

Bill loaded the film into the camera and handed it to Kevin. Outside, Kevin jumped off the porch and turned to see his grandfather slowly coming down the porch stairs.

"Stay there, Grandpa; let me take your picture." Bill stopped in the middle of the staircase. Kevin put his eye to the viewfinder. He focused in on his grandfather, "Wave to me, Grandpa." The old man waved at the camera. "Now, say cheese." The old man mouthed the word, his teeth shown

as a smile. Kevin pressed the button. His view in the viewfinder went black for a second; when it cleared, his grandfather was no longer in the frame. He took the camera from his face. His grandfather was nowhere to be found. "Grandpa, Grandpa, where are you?"

Kevin was afraid to say anything to anyone, so he stayed to himself for the rest of the day. At dinnertime, Linda stood on the porch and called the family home. Everyone came except Grandpa Bill. She called out his name again with no response. Bob went out on his own to look for him. He came back an hour later, alone.

Linda called the police. Five officers combed the area, wielding flashlights. They told Linda how old folks were always wandering off. She told them it was not something she expected from her father. They told her they'd search the roads, north and south, and to keep the phone line open.

At ten o'clock, the police called and told her they'd renew the search in the morning.

Linda sat alone on the porch in her father's chair. She was bent over, crying into her hands. She stopped when she heard someone come out of the house and onto the porch. She looked up; it was Kevin. He handed her a photograph, a black and white, five by seven.

"What's this? Why are you giving this to me?" she asked.

"I thought you'd like to see it."

"This is an old photo, before I was born. That's my parents, your Grandma and Grandpa, that's their friends the Anderson and the Taylors, standing on the steps leading up to this very porch." She examined the photo carefully. "That's strange, if they're all in the picture, who took the photo?"

"I did," said Kevin.

"Don't fool around, Kevin, I'm not in the mood." She looked at the photo again. "Look, they're all smiling and waving hello."

Kevin took the photo and stared back into the house. "They're not waving hello, Mom, they're waving goodbye."

Everybody Has One

BEEN A BUSY, BUSY BUT-BUT BOUNTIFUL YEAR for Shipwreckt Books Publishing Company, which comes to a close none too soon for me with the release of the Solstice 2014 issue of Lost Lake Folk Opera. In the past eighteen months, we have produced twelve original books and magazines, and created an opportunity for fifty authors, poets, essayists, photographers and artisans. Along the way, we've met a lot of fine folks, a few stinkers too, and learned something new almost every day. Can't ask for much more than that; maybe sell more of our beautiful Rocket Science Press, Up On Big Rock Poetry Series and Lost Lake Folk Art books, written, every one of them, by serious, hardworking authors.

The art world – I won't try to define it – publishing included, enjoys the same technological renaissance that has so rapidly changed societies and cultures around the globe. More people have greater access to the ideas of visionaries than ever before. Naturally, the benefits don't come without cost and risk. Don't let the democratization of creativity dull your senses. Don't let smart electronics make you dumb. Don't believe everything you read; listen carefully. Don't let anyone try to tell you what good taste is; and above all, don't fall for watered-down art, brilliance dimmed so that more people will look at it, creativity narrowed by commercial forces until it mimics itself.

Looking forward to a few weeks away from manuscripts and computers, do a little snowshoeing and cross-country skiing with my dogs, old Brother and little Mona.